POWERFUL

To Carrie

Patty McCord

POWERFUL

Building a Culture of
Freedom and Responsibility

| From the Co-Creator of NETFLIX Culture Deck |

Patty McCord

Silicon Guild

Printed in the United States of America

10 9 8 7 6 5 4 3 2 1

Distributed by Publishers Group West
Interior design by Tabitha Lahr

Library of Congress Control Number: 2017913094
ISBN (hardcover): 978-1-939714-09-1
ISBN (ebook): 978-1-939714-11-4
ISBN (international paperback): 978-1-939714-13-8

Published in the United States of America by Silicon Guild, an imprint of Missionday. Bulk purchase discounts, special editions, and customized excerpts are available direct from the publisher. For information about books for educational, business, or promotional purposes, or any other requests, please email: inquiries@missionday.com

Disclaimer: Although the author and publisher have made every effort to ensure that the information in this book was correct at press time, the author and publisher do not assume and hereby disclaim any liability to any party for any loss, damage, or disruption caused by errors or omissions, whether such errors or omissions result from negligence, accident, or any other cause. This book is presented solely for educational and informational purposes. The author and publisher are not offering it as legal, accounting, or other professional services advice. Neither the author nor the publisher shall be held liable or responsible to any person or entity with respect to any loss or incidental or consequential damages caused, or alleged to have been caused, directly or indirectly, by the information or advice contained herein. Every company is different and the advice and strategies contained herein may not be suitable for your situation.

Author's website: www.pattymccord.com

For my dad. The first true leader I knew.

CONTENTS

CHAPTER EIGHT

▶ **The Art of Good Good-byes**
*Make Needed Changes Fast, and Be a Great Place
to Be From* | 124

INTRODUCTION

A New Way of Working

| *Foster Freedom and Responsibility* |

In an executive meeting one day at Netflix, we suddenly realized that in nine months we would account for a third of U.S. Internet bandwidth. We had grown around 30 percent a quarter for three quarters in a row. At the time, we were still thinking that we might eventually be as big as HBO, but not for many years. Our head of product did a quick calculation of how much bandwidth we'd need in a year if we maintained our current growth rate. He then said, "You know, that would be a third of U.S. Internet bandwidth." We all just looked at him and blurted out in unison, "WHAT?" I asked him, "Does anyone at the company know how to make sure we can manage that?" He answered, with the honesty we always hoped for, "I don't know."

In my fourteen years on the executive team at Netflix, we constantly faced such daunting growth challenges, sometimes existential ones, and in technologies and services that we were pioneering. There was no playbook; we had to make it up. From the moment I joined Netflix, when the company had barely launched, the nature of our business and our field of competitors evolved continuously and incredibly rapidly. Our business model, the technology that drove our services, and the teams of people we needed in order to execute had to do more than keep pace—we had to anticipate changes and proactively strategize and prepare for them. We had to hire stellar talent in whole new areas of expertise and fluidly reconfigure our teams. We also had to be ready at any moment to cast aside our plans, admit mistakes, and embrace a new course. The company had to perpetually reinvent itself—first figuring out how to keep our DVD-by-mail business thriving while simultaneously throwing ourselves into learning how to stream; then moving our systems to the cloud; then beginning to create original programming.

This book is not a memoir of the building of Netflix. It is a guide to building a high-performance culture that can meet the challenges of today's rapid pace of change in business, written for team leaders at all levels. Netflix may be an especially stark example, but all companies, from start-ups to corporate behemoths, must become great adapters. They need the ability to anticipate new market demands and to pounce on remarkable opportunities and new technologies. Otherwise, the competition will simply innovate faster. Now that I am consulting with companies all over the world, from large blue chips like J. Walter Thompson to fast-growth newcomers like Warby Parker, HubSpot, and India's Hike Messenger, as well as a number of fledgling start-ups, I see the wider landscape of challenge vividly. It's striking how similar—and pressing—

the fundamental problems are. Everybody wants to know the same thing: how can they create some of their own Netflix mojo? More specifically, how can they create for themselves the kind of nimble, high-performance culture that has made Netflix so successful? That's what this book is about: how you can draw on the lessons that we learned at Netflix and apply the principles and practices we developed to managing your own team or company.

Did we do everything right at Netflix? Not by a long shot. We had plenty of stumbles, some very public. And we didn't have a big aha moment about how to meet our challenges; we evolved a new way of working through incremental adaptation: trying new things, making mistakes, beginning again, and seeing good results. Ultimately, we created a distinctive culture that supports adaptability and high performance. I am not going to claim that tackling the challenges of rapid change is easy in any way or for anyone. The good news is that we found that inculcating a core set of behaviors in people, then giving them the latitude to practice those behaviors—well, actually, demanding that they practice them—makes teams astonishingly energized and proactive. Such teams are the best drivers to get you where you need to go.

I've laced the book with stories about how we met challenges at Netflix, in part to make the book a lively read but also because they show how the methods we developed can be implemented. You will find the book somewhat unconventional—which, I hope you'll agree, is appropriate for a book that is largely about defying convention. One of the pillars of the Netflix culture is radical honesty, something I have loved since I was a small child growing up in straight-talking Texas. If you watch any of my talks that are posted online, you'll see that it's my way to speak freely, and I'm going to do so here. Please think of reading this book like engaging in a lively debate. You may be annoyed by some of what I say and find yourself pushing back on certain points. I hope you'll also find yourself nodding emphatically in agreement with others. As I learned through many intense debates at Netflix, nothing is quite as much fun as a free-flowing intellectual sparring match, and I very much want reading this book to be fun.

People Have Power; Don't Take It Away

The first step in adopting the practices I'll present is embracing a management mind-set that overturns conventional wisdom.

The fundamental lesson we learned at Netflix about success in business today is this: the elaborate, cumbersome system for managing people that was developed over the course of the twentieth century is just not up to the challenges companies face in the twenty-first. Reed Hastings and I and the rest of the management team decided that, over time, we would explore a radical new way to manage people—a way that would allow them to exercise their full powers.

We wanted all of our people to challenge us, and one another, vigorously. We wanted them to speak up about ideas and problems; to freely push back, in front of one another and in front of us. We didn't want anyone, at any level, keeping vital insights and concerns to themselves. The executive team modeled this: We made ourselves accessible, and we encouraged questions. We engaged in open, intense debate and made sure all of our managers knew we wanted them to do the same. Reed even staged debates between members of the executive team. We also communicated honestly and continuously about challenges the company was facing and how we were going to tackle them. We wanted everyone to understand that change would be a constant and that we would make what-ever changes of plan, and of personnel, we thought necessary to forge ahead at high speed. We wanted people to embrace the need for change and be thrilled to drive it. We had come to understand that the most successful organizations in this world of increasingly rapid disruption will be the ones in which everyone, on every team, understands that all bets are off and everything is changing—and thinks that's great.

To build that kind of company, we were intent on creat-ing a culture of great teamwork and innovative problem solv-ing. We wanted people to feel excited to come to work each day, not despite the challenges but because of them. I'm not going to say that working at Netflix wasn't often extremely hair-raising. Some of the decisions we had to make were radi-cal plunges into the unknown, and that was often truly scary. But it was also exhilarating.

The Netflix culture wasn't built by developing an elab-orate new system for managing people; we did the opposite. We kept stripping away policies and procedures. We realized that the prevailing approach to building teams and managing people is as outdated as product innovation was before the quickening pace of disruption demanded the development of agile, lean, and customer-centric methods. It's not that com-panies aren't trying all kinds of things to manage better; but most of what they're doing is either beside the point or coun-terproductive.

Most companies are clinging to the established com-mand-and-control system of top-down decision making but trying to jazz it up by fostering "employee engagement" and by "empowering" people. Compelling but misguided ideas about "best practices" prevail: bonuses and pay tied to annual performance reviews; big HR initiatives like the recent craze for lifelong learning programs; celebrations to build camaraderie and make sure people have some fun; and, for employees who are struggling, performance improvement plans. These foster empowerment, and with that comes engagement, which leads to job satisfaction and employee happiness, and that leads to high performance, or so the thinking goes.

I used to believe this too. I started my career in HR at Sun Microsystems and then Borland Software, implementing the whole gamut of conventional practices. I negotiated all kinds of tantalizing bonuses. I dutifully rallied my teams for the dreaded performance review season and coached managers through the performance improvement process. When I ran diversity programs at Sun, I even spent $100,000 on a Cinco de Mayo party. But over time I saw that all of those policies and systems were enormously costly, time-consuming, and unproductive. Even more important, I saw that they were premised on false assumptions about human beings: that most people must be incentivized in order to really throw themselves into their work, and that they need to be told what to do. The "best practices" that have been developed on the basis of these premises are, ironically, disincentivizing and disempowering.

Yes, engaged employees probably deliver higher-quality performance, but too often engagement is treated as the endgame, rather than serving customers and getting results. And the standard beliefs about how and why people are engaged in their work miss the true drivers of work passion. As for empowerment, I simply hate that word. The idea is well intentioned, but the truth is that there is so much concern about empowering people only because the prevailing way of managing them takes their power away. We didn't set out to take it away; we just overprocessed everything. We've hamstrung people.

What I came to understand deeply and in a new way once

I made my way into the scrappier start-up world is that people *have* power. A company's job isn't to empower people; it's to remind people that they walk in the door with power and to create the conditions for them to exercise it. Do that, and you will be astonished by the great work they will do for you.

Managing People Like Managing Innovation

As I introduce the alternative management methods we developed at Netflix, I'm going to challenge all of the basic premises of management today: that it is about building loyalty and retention and career progression and implementing structures to ensure employee engagement and happiness. None of that is true. None of this is the job of management.

Here is my radical proposition: a business leader's job is to create great teams that do amazing work on time. That's it. That's the job of management.

At Netflix we did away with virtually all of the hidebound policies and procedures. We didn't do it in one fell swoop. We did it experimentally, step by step, over the course of years. We approached developing the culture in the same way we approached innovating the business. I understand that such a radical transformation is simply not feasible for some companies. And many team leaders are not free to do away with policies and procedures. But every company and every manager *is* free to institute the practices we used to instill the core set of behaviors that made the Netflix culture so limber.

The Discipline of Freedom and Responsibility

Doing away with policies and procedures and giving people agency didn't at all mean that the culture became a free-for-all.

As we stripped away bureaucracy, we coached all of our people, at all levels and on all teams, to be disciplined about a fundamental set of behaviors. I've often said that while I've removed the words "policy" and "procedure" from my vocabulary, I love discipline. My whole career I have gotten along well with engineers, because engineers are very, very disciplined. When engineers start to whine about a process you're trying to implement, you want to really dig into what's bothering them, because they hate senseless bureaucracy and stupid process. But they don't mind discipline at all.

The most important thing to understand about transforming a culture, whether that of a team or a whole company, is that it isn't a matter of simply professing a set of values and operating principles. It's a matter of identifying the behaviors that you would like to see become consistent practices and then instilling the discipline of actually *doing* them. We fully and consistently communicated to everyone at Netflix the behaviors we expected them to be disciplined about, and that started with the executive team and every manager. We were so intent that every single employee understand our philosophy and the behaviors we wanted them to execute on that Reed started writing a PowerPoint about them, which I and many other members of the management team also contributed to. It ultimately became known as the Netflix Culture Deck. You may have read it.

When Reed posted it on the Web several years ago, he had no idea it would go viral, with more than fifteen million views and counting. We hadn't created it for broadcast. We created it as an internal company document, using it to communicate the culture to new hires and make sure we were perfectly clear about how we wanted them to operate. We also stressed that it laid out not only what we expected of them but also what they should expect of us. The Deck wasn't written in one fell swoop and it wasn't written just by Reed and me. It was a living, breathing, growing, changing set of realizations we came to as we built the culture, with leaders from all around the company making contributions. Reading the Deck would be a great complement to reading this book, and one reason I've written this book is that I get so many questions when I speak and in my consulting about the Deck and how to actually enact its concepts.

I've thought hard about that, and I have boiled down the lessons we learned about how to instill these principles and behaviors in teams. Not all of the specific practices implemented at Netflix and outlined in the Deck apply to every team or company. Even at Netflix, the culture varied in many respects from department to department. Marketing, for example, was run in many ways that were quite different from the management of the engineering groups. But there was a core set of practices that underpinned the culture:

- We wanted open, clear, and constant communication about the work to be done and the challenges being faced, not only for a manager's own team but for the company as a whole.

- We wanted people to practice radical honesty: telling one another, and us, the truth in a timely fashion and ideally face to face.

- We wanted people to have strong, fact-based opinions and to debate them avidly and test them rigorously.

- We wanted people to base their actions on what was best for the customer and the company, not on attempts to prove themselves right.

- We wanted hiring managers to take the lead in preparing their teams for the future by making sure they had high performers with the right skills in every position.

We asked all managers, starting at the top with our executive team, to model these behaviors, and by doing so, they showed everyone on their teams how to embrace them as well.

The prospect of getting teams to operate according to these requirements may seem daunting. More than a few Netflixers I've talked with as I've worked on this book have commented that they were reluctant about one or another of the practices, such as giving totally honest feedback to people face to face. They have also recalled that as they forced themselves to go ahead, they saw how responsive their people were and how dramatically their team's performance improved. The key is to proceed incrementally. You can start with small steps and then keep building. Pick a practice that you think fits your group and business issues particularly well and start there. For leadership teams, start with one department or group you think is best suited or most in need of change. Creating a culture is an evolutionary process. Think of it as an experimental journey of discovery. That was how we thought about building the culture at Netflix. Which step you start with is no matter; what matters is starting. With the pace of change in business today, there is, as the saying goes, no time like the present.

CHAPTER ONE

The Greatest Motivation Is Contributing to Success

| Treat People Like Adults |

Great teams are made when every single member knows where they're going and will do anything to get there. Great teams are not created with incentives, procedures, and perks. They are created by hiring talented people who are adults and want nothing more than to tackle a challenge, and then communicating to them, clearly and continuously, about what the challenge is.

The prevailing philosophy of management today is that if you want great productivity from people, you must first motivate them with incentives and then make sure they know you're looking over their shoulders to keep them accountable. So many companies have department objectives and team objectives and individual objectives and a formal annual review process for measuring performance against them. That structure, that waterfall, is very logical, very reasonable. But it's no longer remotely adequate. Saying to employees, "If you do X, you'll be rewarded with Y," assumes a static system. Yet no business today is static. More fundamentally, while rewards are great, there is no better reward than making a significant contribution to meeting a challenge.

I'm a big fan of goals. Couldn't be a bigger fan. It's the usual management approach to achieving them that is so wrong. Typically, the time frames we set and the complexity of the structure created for leading teams and monitoring results make achieving goals harder than it needs to be.

Great Teams Relish a Challenge

When I consult to start-ups, I'm most excited about working with those who've found that their venture money is starting to dry up and they're facing really tough challenges; it's tackling those that makes truly great teams. Great teams are made when things are hard. Great teams are made when you have to dig deep. When I'm hiring, I look for someone who gets really excited about the problems we have to solve. You want them to wake up in the morning thinking, *God, this is hard. I want to do this!* Being given a great problem to tackle and the right colleagues to tackle it with is the best incentive of all. One of my mantras is "Problem finders, they're cheap!" Most people think that's a really important role in the company: *I'm the one who found that problem!* Okay, good for you, but did you solve it? You want people who absolutely love problem solving.

Neil Blumenthal and Dave Gilboa, cofounders of Warby Parker, told me that it's especially fun building the company now because it's getting really complicated as they launch brick-and-mortar stores. They've got to integrate the experience of the stores with the experience of the online service, and that's a real challenge. No wonder the brand is so successful. Some leaders might opt to coast on the growth already achieved, but they're thrilled to be facing even harder problems.

Ask any very successful person what their fondest memories of their career are, and they will inevitably tell you about an early period of struggle or some remarkably difficult challenge they had to overcome. I had a great conversation about this with Tom Willerer, the former VP of product innovation at Netflix. He's moved over to Coursera, the innovative online education provider, as chief product officer. When I asked him what he's loved about helping build the company, he lit up, launching into a story about a seemingly impossible feat his team pulled off. At the start of the fiscal year, the executive team had determined that the company had to double its revenue by the end of the year. He and the product team decided they'd meet the goal by launching fifty new courses by that September, which he described as a Hail Mary pass. Two weeks before the launch date for the new courses, they still weren't sure they could pull it off. They did, and the strategy worked beautifully. They saw an immediate hockey-stick uptick in earnings. Tom told me he joined a company that he wasn't sure would even exist in five years because of the "hunger to climb a mountain." He said, "I feel sometimes like I'm going to lose a limb doing this, but it will be worth it because I'm doing something important and adding something to the world, and that is what drives people." I could not agree with him more. I believe that is the way that most people fervently want to feel about their work.

The prospect of helping to create a company that would

provide employees that opportunity was the reason I joined Netflix, despite thinking I wouldn't go to another start-up.

When I got a call at two in the morning back in 1997, I figured it must be Reed Hastings. Nobody else ever called me at two in the morning.

He said, "Were you sleeping?" And I said, "Yeah, of course I was. I'm normal! What's up?"

Reed was not one to let a little sleep get in the way of a good idea, and he had shared many of them with me late at night when I worked with him at his start-up Pure Software. After he sold Pure, he'd gone back to school and I had started consulting. We both lived in the same town and we'd kept in close touch.

He said that he was going to join Netflix, and I told him, "Sounds like a good career move. Why are you telling me this at two in the morning?"

Then he asked me if I wanted to join him and I answered, "No way." I'd had a great time at Pure, but I was done with the crazy highs and lows and insane hours. I also didn't see how a tiny little company renting DVDs through the mail was going to succeed. I mean, really, Netflix was going to put Blockbuster out of business?!

But then Reed said, "Wouldn't it be great if we created a company that we really both wanted to work at?" Now I was intrigued. At Pure I'd come in after the model had been fashioned. The opportunity to join in the invention this time was tantalizing.

"If we did that," I asked him, "how would you know it was great?"

He said, "Oh, I'd want to come to work every day and solve *these* problems with *these* people."

I loved the spirit of that. I think Reed expressed in that

statement exactly what people most want from work: to be able to come in and work with the right team of people—colleagues they trust and admire—and to focus like crazy on doing a great job together.

Policies and Structure Can't Anticipate Needs and Opportunities

If you look at the most successful companies of the last decade or so, many of them are Internet firms with teams that work very collaboratively and organically. What do I mean by organically? I mean their goals and the ways they allocate time and resources, as well as the problems they're focusing on and approaches to solving them, are constantly adapting to the demands of the business and customer. They are growing, changing organisms. They aren't rigid structures bound by predetermined mandates about objectives, staff, or budget.

Before Netflix, I worked for Reed at Pure Software, which was my first start-up job, and I felt like I'd died and gone to heaven. I loved the high energy and the intense focus on innovation. As the head of HR, I still introduced policies and procedures, but I began doubting the conventional wisdom. Because the company was so much smaller than others I'd worked at, I began to learn more about the nitty-gritty of the business, and I could get to know more employees. As I became familiar with software engineers, in particular, and observed how they work, I realized that it's a misconception that more people make better stuff. With our teams at Pure, and all around Silicon Valley, I could see the power of small, unencumbered teams.

The typical approach to growth in business is to add more people and structure and to impose more fixed budgetary goals and restraints. But my experiences at fast-growth companies that successfully scaled showed me that the leanest processes possible and a strong culture of discipline were far superior, if for no other reason than their speed.

Later, at Netflix, we had a striking realization about this after we had a big, very painful layoff. In 2001 we had to lay off a third of the company. The dot-com bubble had burst, and the economy had gone bust with it, and we were on the brink of bankruptcy. It was brutal. Then that Christmas the cost of DVD players dropped and they became the big gift, and the business took off. Now we had to do twice the work with two thirds the people. We couldn't hire anybody except people to put DVDs in envelopes. We had so many new customers that we didn't have enough inventory, and we had to put every tiny cent of profit we had into buying more product. And yet everyone was much happier. I was carpooling to work with Reed one day, and I said to him, "Why is this so fun? I can't wait to get to work. I don't want to go home at night. We're working so hard, but it's great. What is it about what we're doing?" He said, "Let's figure it out."

Our first big realization was that the remaining people were the highest performers, and it taught us that the best thing you can do for employees is hire only high performers to work alongside them. It's a perk far better than foosball or free sushi or even a big signing bonus or the holy grail of stock options. Excellent colleagues, a clear purpose, and well-understood deliverables: that's the powerful combination.

When I Saw the Light

Reed and I and the executive team were determined to figure out how to sustain the creative spirit and extraordinary level of performance our teams were demonstrating as the company rapidly scaled up. We were going to have to start hiring *fast*, and we wanted to ensure that we maintained our exceptionally high talent density—the high quotient of top performers that had seen us through the downturn so deftly. We began to systematically explore how we could free people up to do their best work while also providing the right amount of guidance and feedback to keep teams on track yet able to dramatically change course if necessary.

This was when I learned in a much deeper way about the drivers of high-performance innovation. For the first time in my career, as a member of the executive team, I was directly engaged in developing the product itself. It wasn't a highly technical, complex software product, as at Pure. We were an entertainment company, and I was a huge movie fan. I was also, as I would say often to tweak the engineers, *normal*. I was the customer. I became fascinated with how we were developing the product. We were huge fans of A/B testing, rigorous experimentation, and open debate about what was right for the product. In product development, if something doesn't work, you get rid of it. I realized we could apply that same principle to managing people.

I understood that part of the reason large teams are crippled in their ability to innovate and move fast is that because it's hard work to manage them, companies build infrastructure to make sure people are doing the right things. But the teams I saw that accomplished great stuff just knew what they most needed to accomplish; they didn't need elaborate procedures, and certainly not incentives. Most technologists will tell you that a small team of brilliant engineers will do better work than a large team of hardworking ones. I started thinking: Why would that be true just for engineers? Is it because they are so special and smart? At that time, much as I love engineers, I was pretty tired of their being treated as the special, smart people. To my mind, people across the full spectrum of functions would love nothing more than to be free to tackle projects in the way they think will produce the best results in the shortest possible time. So often, though, they are thwarted by management second-guessing them or by inefficient systems. I wondered: what if people in marketing and finance and my own group, human resources, were allowed to unleash their full powers? They would operate like high-performance engineering teams. In retrospect, that was the moment I left behind traditional HR and took on a new role as the COO of culture and the chief product manager of people.

I began to scrutinize our organizational structure and design. At that point, we had created departments, and Reed and I had agreed that as much as we could, we wanted to keep their management flat because that gave us so much speed. After we'd had to let many middle managers go in our big layoff, we had noticed that everyone moved much faster without all those layers of opinions and approvals. Now we decided that maybe people could move even faster and get more done if we started doing away with policies and procedures. We analyzed every single truism and best practice, just as we analyzed the product. Often when Reed would propose a cut, it sounded so crazy I needed to sleep on it. But as we kept trying things, we kept getting good results. Take our no-vacation-policy policy, which has received a great deal of press. We told people to take the time they thought was appropriate, just discussing what they needed with their managers. And do you know what happened? People took a week or two in the summer and time for the holidays and some days here and there to watch their kids' ball games, just as before. Trusting people to be responsible with their time was one of the early steps in giving them back their power.

I discovered I loved throwing away convention. One of my favorite days was when I stood up in front of the company and said, "I'm going to get rid of our expense policy and I'm going to get rid of the travel policy, and I want you to just use good judgment about how you spend the company's money. If it turns out to be a disaster, like the lawyers tell us it will, we'll go back to the old system." Again we found that people didn't abuse the freedom. We saw that we could treat people like adults and that they loved it.

I started to challenge the conventions around hiring people too. With the company growing like mad and the nature of the business changing so fast—we could see streaming rapidly approaching—we knew we had to build an organization that would always have a really strong talent pipeline. At the time, when I hired a manager, they typically wanted to work with their favorite headhunter, and I knew I had to change that. We needed to be more strategic. I could have tried to get the five best headhunters in Silicon Valley to work for me exclusively. But I decided to throw out the traditional recruiting practice and create a headhunting firm within the company. Instead of hiring people who had worked in other companies internally, I started hiring people who'd worked for headhunting firms to build that capability inside. Because we had that competency, I could tell a manager, "It's okay if you lose a couple of people, because we can get great new people for you fast."

We also challenged the conventional practices for crafting both company-wide and team strategy. We had been creating an annual road map and doing annual budgeting, but those processes took so much time, and the effort wasn't worthwhile because we were wrong all the time. I mean, really, we were making it up. Whatever our projections were, we knew they would be wrong in six months, if not three. So we just stopped doing annual planning. All the time we saved gave us more time to do quarterly planning, and then we went to rolling three-quarter budgets, because that was as far out as we thought we could ostensibly predict.

We experimented with every way we could think of to liberate teams from unnecessary rules and approvals. As we kept methodically analyzing what was working and how we could keep freeing people to be more creative, productive, and happy, we came to refer to our new way of working as the freedom and responsibility culture. We worked for years to develop it—and the evolution continues today. I'll describe the additional components in the chapters to come. They were all built upon the realization that the most important job of management is to focus really intently on the building of great teams. If you hire the talented people you need, and you provide them with the tools and information they need to get you where you need to go, they will want nothing more than to do stellar work for you and keep you limber.

The most recent testament to the power of this approach is the speed with which Netflix has expanded its original programming while also achieving popular and critical success. Ted Sarandos, head of content since the earliest days, told me that freeing high performers from constraints has been vital to building up the original-content business so rapidly. The team has doubled their creation of new content every year, and when we talked, they were producing thirty scripted series and had twelve feature films, fifty-five documentary projects, fifty-one stand-up comedy shows, and forty-five children's shows in production. On top of that, they had just gone global, expanding to thirteen countries at once. What's so amazing is not only the speed with which the team has created so much content but also the diversity of types of content. Ted's group has been able to cater to all sorts of tastes, with offerings ranging from highbrow series like *The Crown* to the wildly crowd-pleasing but hardly critically acclaimed *Fuller House*. The team has even entered the fray of unscripted series, such as with *Ultimate Beastmaster*, a competition show with contestants from six different countries, each speaking their own language.

Ted says that his core approach has been asking his team to focus on finding the best creative talent with the skills to execute, and then giving those creators the freedom to realize their vision. That has been the greatest differentiator between Netflix and the Hollywood studios, he says, allowing his team to compete so effectively for top creative talent and to launch such breakthrough shows. Creators love that his team doesn't micromanage the production process, barraging them with notes. Ted's group also doesn't use the traditional pilot system, instead green-lighting creators to produce a full season of episodes. They put their confidence in people who've proven they can produce, and hand in hand with the freedom those people are given is the understanding that it's they who are accountable for the quality of shows. They have risen to the occasion. By contrast, the traditional Hollywood way has been creation by committee, with accountability spread too thin.

Ted told me that being steeped in the Netflix culture also allowed him to feel comfortable freeing his team from constraints they might have imposed on themselves. For example, they broke their own model for bringing in new shows with only their third original series. Because they weren't using pilot testing, they had decided to bring in only series that already had very well-developed scripts and the acting talent lined up. But then Jenji Kohan, the creator of the Showtime series *Weeds*, proposed *Orange Is the New Black* before any scripts were written. Ted and his team were so impressed by her vision for the show and had such confidence based on her track record with *Weeds* that they very shrewdly threw their rule out.

• • •

Ask yourself: If you were to treat managing people the way you treat managing product, wouldn't you also want to approach the entire system differently? If you started not with best practices but with what it takes to deliver a fabulous end product to your customers, what system would you invent? Wouldn't you want your people to be more agile? Wouldn't you want to be able to rely on their being proactive and staying ahead of the curve, because they know that they've got to help you steer the way? Wouldn't you rather be devoting the full measure of your time and attention to making sure they have the resources and information they need to do that for you and to discussing challenges with them, getting their best input and their pushback, rather than processing forms and approvals and policing them?

I'm not at all saying that teams don't need direction setting and coaching. They do. But the ways in which they're given direction and feedback are often far from optimal. At the same time we were experimenting at Netflix with eliminating processes, we were also experimenting with better ways of communicating where the company was heading, what goals to be driving toward, and how people were performing.

IN BRIEF

▶ The greatest team achievements are driven by all team members understanding the ultimate goal and being free to creatively problem-solve in order to get there.

▶ The strongest motivator is having great team members to work with, people who trust one another to do great work and to challenge one another.

▶ The most important job of managers is to ensure that all team members are such high performers who do great work and challenge one another.

▶ You should operate with the leanest possible set of policies, procedures, rules, and approvals, because most of these top-down mandates hamper speed and agility.

▶ Discover how lean you can go by steadily experimenting. If it turns out a policy or procedure was needed, reinstate it. Constantly seek to refine your culture just as you constantly work to improve your products and services.

QUESTIONS TO CONSIDER

- As you survey your company-wide policies and procedures, ask: What is the purpose of this policy or procedure? Does it achieve that result?

- Are there any approval mechanisms you can eliminate?

- What percentage of its time does management spend on problem solving and team building?

- Have you done a cost-benefit analysis of the incentives and perks you offer employees?

- Could you replace approvals and permissions with analysis of spending patterns and a focus on accuracy and predictability?

- Is your decision-making system clear and communicated widely?

CHAPTER TWO

Every Single Employee Should Understand the Business

| *Communicate Constantly About the Challenge* |

When I advise doing away with as many procedures and approvals as possible, I am inevitably asked, "But how? How can that be possible? What takes the place of rules, processes, approvals, bureaucracy, and permissions?" The answer: Clear, continuous communication about the context of the work to be done. Telling people, "Here's exactly where we are, and here's what we're trying to accomplish." The more time managers spend communicating and elaborating and being transparent about the job to be done, about the challenges the business is facing and the larger competitive context, the less important policies, approvals, and incentives are.

Even if you're not at liberty to do away with policies, procedures, bonuses, and formal annual reviews, you can implement much clearer, more open, honest, and continuous communication about the business challenges and how employees are meeting them. This facilitates much more timely improvements in performance as well as more limber adjustments of goals. It also encourages people to ask questions and share ideas, which can lead to extremely valuable insights about how to improve your product, your service to your customers, and the business itself. I came to appreciate how important it is for every single employee to truly understand the business when I myself began to learn deeply about the business at Netflix.

People Don't Want to Be Entertained at Work; They Want to Learn

When I was at Sun we had 370 people in HR. 370 people! And virtually all of them were divorced from the business; they couldn't tell you what we made. We were doing initiatives and off-sites and celebrations. We were half entertainment and half happy-face HR. It was really fun but somehow empty. We always wanted more respect and recognition.

I became jazzed about my work in a new way when I became integrally involved in growing the company at Netflix. When I accepted the job, it was on the condition that I would not be siloed off as the HR lady; I would report directly to Reed and be part of the executive team. That meant that I had to step up and learn deeply about how the business worked. As I did that, I came to understand the enormous value of every single employee at the company gaining the same understanding. Reed and I had both been inspired by the argument

for open-book management in Jack Stack and Bo Burling-
ham's book *The Great Game of Business*. The importance of
transparency was driven home for me by our dramatic shift
from the DVD-by-mail model to the subscription model.

One morning when Reed and I were carpooling to work,
he started passionately talking about changing from a pay-
per-rental service to a subscription model, getting all fired up
about it. I told him, "Okay, all right! I can hear it in your
voice. I know what happens when you get like this. You are
sure you're right about this, aren't you?" I knew that most
employees weren't going to like the change, but I also knew
that Reed was going to do it anyway because he believed
it was the right thing for the business. It was clear that the
change would be wrenching. It involved much more than simply changing the terms on the website; we had to change the
shipping model and the billing model and the whole structure
of the company, its departments and supervisors and salespeople. We also had to bring in lots of new people who could
build up our technical capabilities for serving subscribers and
making good use of the tsunami of user data we'd be accumu-
lating, and we were facing intense competition for them from
our biggest competitor, which was a hundred times bigger
than we were: Blockbuster.

The beautiful thing for me was that because the shift in
the business was so dramatic, I had to focus very intensively
on two things. First, I had to deeply understand the new business model and what was at stake. Subscription is a numbers
race, and revenue occurs only over time after an up-front
investment. I appreciated what a very big bet it was. We'd
have to spend considerable money to sign up a first group of
subscribers, which was an investment in getting more customers, and those new customers would allow us to pay for the

next expansion. This is the fundamental Netflix model; pay up front for benefits in future years. At this stage in our growth, that considerable up-front expense meant that we didn't have much time to make the model work. Second, the urgency of getting it right meant that I had to help everyone else in the company understand the new business model too. At the time, the only model any of us knew included due dates and late fees. When Reed proposed a subscription without due dates and late fees, it was truly scary. After all, late fees were the gas in Blockbuster's engine. When we said weren't going to charge them, everybody in the company was asking, "How's that going to work?"

I fell in love with being a businessperson, and I didn't want to be happy-face HR den mother anymore. I also fell in love with explaining very clearly and fully to everyone in the company why we were making the decisions we were, how they could best participate in achieving our goals, and what the obstacles would be.

My aha moment reminded me of when my son was six and playing soccer. My husband was the coach, and I'd go to lots of the practices. Watching the kids was hysterical. They'd just clump around the ball. I asked my husband in the car on the way to the team's first game, "So what's your strategy for the game?" He said, "Well, I was going to really attempt to have everybody moving down the field in the same direction at the same time." I responded, "You know, I think that's achievable," and he said, "Well, but in the second half, they've got to go the other way." The World Cup fell later in the season, and I had the kids over to watch. When they saw the view of the game from the blimp, they realized, *Oh! That's what a pass looks like!* Business is no different.

People need to see the view from the C suite in order to

feel truly connected to the problem solving that must be done at all levels and on all teams, so that the company is spotting issues and opportunities in every corner of the business and effectively acting on them. The irony is that companies have invested so much in training programs of all sorts and spent so much time and effort to incentivize and measure performance, but they've failed to actually explain to all of their employees how their business runs.

The Heartbeat of Communication

Of course, as a business grows more complex, communicating about how it works, let alone about the course for the future, also becomes more complicated. Working out how to do this—and, for company leaders and HR executives, coaching all managers to do it, and do it consistently and continuously—takes time. The key is to establish what I call a strong heartbeat of communication, and that takes experimentation and practice.

For a time, Reed and I would meet with every ten new hires in a room and go through a PowerPoint, which was our starting point in creating the Culture Deck. We'd say, "This is your cheat sheet. This is what you should expect from one another and absolutely expect from your management." Over time, we developed "new employee college." For one whole day each quarter, every head of every department would make an hourlong presentation on the important issues and developments in their part of the business. The idea for the college actually came from Cindy Holland, who is now VP of content acquisition/original series. She and I were backstage watching a set of management presentations the executive team was giving to a group of investors. She realized that she was learning a great deal, and she turned to me and asked, "Why do we do all of this hard work for a bunch of strangers but don't do it for ourselves?" So we rolled it out for everybody.

Netflixers will recall with a kind of awe that taking in all the information at new employee college was like drinking from a fire hose. They heard detailed presentations that included the metrics and the deliverables of each department. This not only gave employees a deep understanding of our business but also introduced them to the heads of the different parts of the business. Better still, they could ask those people questions.

Ensure That Communication Flows Both Up and Down

It's vital that communication go both ways. People must be able to ask questions and offer critiques and ideas. Ideally, they should be able to do so with all managers, up to the CEO. At new employee college, as we started the proceedings, we'd say to the participants, "You will take out of this day what you put into it. If you don't ask questions, you won't get answers." I look back now and realize that this was crucial early stage-setting for the success of the company. It gave people at all levels license to freely ask for clarification, whether about something they were expected to do or about a decision made by management. Not only did this mean they were better informed, but over time it instilled throughout the company a culture of curiosity. That meant managers often gained important insights because someone had asked a really good question. Here's a great example. During new employee college, Ted Sarandos explained what's called windowing of content. The term refers to the traditional system that developed for feature film distribution: a movie would first come out in theaters, then go to hotels, then to DVD, and at that point Netflix could bid to pick it up. During the Q&A, an engineer asked Ted, "Why does the windowing of content happen like that? It seems stupid." Ted recalls that the question stopped him cold. He realized that although it was the convention, he really didn't know why, and he answered frankly, "I don't know." He told me that the question stuck with him and that it "made me challenge everything about the windowing of content, and years later, it contributed to my complete comfort with releasing all episodes of a series at once, even though no one had ever done that in television."

Never underestimate the value of the ideas, and the questions, that employees at all levels may surprise you with.

Everyone Working for You, at All Levels, Can Understand Your Business

I expect you've had the experience of talking to someone on your team about a business issue and being asked a question that makes you think, *This person is* clueless! Well, next time it happens, I want you to say to yourself, *Wait, right, this person is clueless. He doesn't know what I know. So I have to inform him.*

When I would talk with a team leader at Netflix about a team member who needed more help understanding a problem—which, given the fast-moving and technical nature of so much of the business, happened regularly—sometimes I'd get pushback. They'd say something like "I tried to explain it to him but he's too stupid to listen." My answer was always "Well, then you made it too complicated to understand." The rule I would give them was this: explain it as though you're explaining to your mother. This was because often through the years, when I'd talk to my mom about some HR initiative I was spearheading, speaking fluent HR gobbledygook, she'd say to me, "Honey, that just sounds stupid." She was always right.

Coming up with simple yet robust ways to explain every aspect of the business isn't easy, but it pays huge rewards. To drive this home when I consult, I often ask managers of companies with a customer service group, "How much do you think your customer service representatives understand about how your business works? Do they appreciate the most pressing issues facing the business? How much do you think they know about how their work contributes to the bottom line—and I mean really know, meaning the numbers?"

Now, how often do you think companies drop the ball when it comes to customer service, despite all the talk about improving the customer experience? The research offers a wealth of appalling data. Reportedly 78 percent of consumers have failed to complete a purchase or other transaction because of a poor service experience, and the costs to businesses in the United States have been estimated at $62 billion annually. Research also shows that word of bad customer experiences spreads to twice as many people as that of good experiences. This is a problem that must still by and large be solved by people. Despite attempts to offer customer service through computer bots or preprogrammed FAQs or messaging systems, face-to-face or voice-to-voice service is far and away most effective.

Any company with a customer service organization wants those people to be highly engaged, and the first step is to teach them how to read the company's P&L. Of course, generally they are the last people the P&L would be shown to. After all, most of them don't stay long, right? They're the lowest on the totem pole. Yet all business success is fundamentally driven by word-of-mouth marketing, and the people who are in direct contact with customers must understand that their every inter-action with a customer leads to that person telling another per-son, for free, either to use the company's product or service or not to. Everyone in customer service, from day one, should understand exactly how the experience they provide customers directly impacts the bottom line. Making that clear isn't diffi-cult. Every company has calculated its cost of customer acqui-sition, and each person who becomes a customer on another customer's recommendation saves the company that amount of money. Every company can share that information with ser-vice representatives as part of bringing them on board.

When I give this advice about sharing business details, I sometimes get the response that only smart people can under-stand this information and only smart people want it. I find that there's a bias among executives that this is "MBA stuff" and that "those people" wouldn't be interested or couldn't get it. My answer: then don't hire people who are that stupid. Bet-ter yet, don't assume that people *are* stupid. Assume instead that if they are doing stupid things, they are either uninformed or misinformed.

But surely employees need to be at a higher level before they're told so much about the down and dirty of the business, no? What if the department is in trouble? What if the com-pany is struggling to build a market for a big new product? Won't they be freaked out? And can they really be trusted with so much information? Of course, some information must be kept private, but you can absolutely convey the intensity of the competition you're up against and share the major chal-lenges being faced.

It's ironic how little information about strategy, opera-tions, and results is generally shared with employees throughout companies. After all, public companies share that information with the whole world these days. Why should the investors on earnings calls know more about what's happening in your business than most of the people working in it? I think it would be great if companies held the equivalent of an earnings call for all employees. In fact, why not have them listen to the actual earnings calls?

If your people aren't informed by you, there's a good chance they'll be misinformed by others. If you don't tell them about how the business is doing, what your strategy is, the challenges you're facing, and what market analysts think of how you're doing, then they will get that information elsewhere—either from colleagues, who will often be equally ill informed, or from the Web, which loves nothing so much as a rumor of doom or a juicy conspiracy theory.

Team Coaches Are the Model, Not Guidance Counselors, Professors, or Entertainers

So many companies spend so much money on—and ask employees to devote so much time away from their jobs for—formal training classes. Much of this time, money, and effort is misplaced. As sports coaches will tell you, there's no better way to learn how to perform than to be in the game.

A little while back I was consulting to a young company I love, and the learning and development head told me that their younger people needed to learn to be better managers. I asked, "What do they need to know how to do?" She answered, "Well, they need to be better managers." I said, "Specifically doing what?" And she said, "Management." I pressed, "But what part?" She responded, "Well, we're going to have to have a full curriculum with conflict management and interpersonal communication." Those are probably the two most popular classes in the training canon, and I'm sure they've helped some people become better managers. But if I could pick one course to teach everybody in the company, whether they're in management or not, it would be on the fundamentals of how the business works and serving customers. This is the information people most want, because they know they can take it and run with it. Courses on conflict resolution they generally roll their eyes about, not to mention resenting the time away from their work.

What about the so-called millennials? I get asked all the time in my consulting, "You know we have to treat millennials differently. What is your advice?" People have gotten the impression that millennials require perks and all sorts of lifelong learning programs, because surveys show that what they most want from their work is to keep learning. I think it's totally false that we have to treat them differently. I can't stand the term "millennials," and the ones I know hate the name tag too. We should simply think of them as people early in their careers. Yes, we should teach them more, but we should teach them more about how business works. It's great that they want to learn. How could they not? They're just out of school. They're in that spongy, want-to-learn-everything phase of life. They're going to eat up whatever you feed them. If it's just snacks, that's all they're going to eat. But if you start feeding their brains the real meat of business, you'll be amazed by how engaged they are and by how much they contribute. They are not some sort of alien being. They are young workers bursting with potential. If we teach young employees how to read a P&L instead of how to tap a beer keg, or give them an honest-to-God project they have to collaborate on rather than doing an online training about collaboration, we're giving them a skill they will apply for the rest of their lives. They understand what constitutes true lifelong learning.

As for perks and entertainment, sure, people like them. Who doesn't enjoy some free pizza or cocktails with colleagues? I sure do. But I've found that the best perks and special time away from the grind are opportunities to understand the business and customers better. At Netflix in the early days, we created many opportunities for people to learn about the movie business. Many of us were film nuts, but we didn't know much about how films get made or about the culture of true film fanatics, and at that time Netflix was especially well known to that crowd for offering art films that were hard to find anywhere else. So we took the whole company to the Sundance Film Festival. We also regularly brought people down to Los Angeles to hear talks by famous directors and cinematographers and editors. I was a huge fan of off-sites too, but not for having good barbecue. We planned serious agendas and had people present lots of data, pose really tough questions, and debate like crazy about the company's future and the competitive landscape.

When I got a call last winter to talk at a gathering of five hundred software engineers at a dude ranch in eastern Washington, I couldn't wait to hop on the plane for some quality time with my beloved geeks. The meeting was all about the future of artificial intelligence. Spending three days immersed in everything to think and know about how the most game-changing technology of our time will transform every service and product on the planet? What could be better?

You may not be able to sponsor such a gathering, or to send yourself and your team to one, but think about everything you can do with the resources you have to provide them with as much information as you can that will help them help you better.

Keep At It Constantly

At Netflix we all thought at first that we'd just do a simple little slide deck and pull it out again and again. As it turned out, not only did every new batch of employees have different questions, but the nature of the business and the challenges kept changing. You've got to constantly monitor the message and update it. This is a job that you should be doing forever.

How do you know when people are well enough informed? Here's my measure. If you stop any employee, at any level of the company, in the break room or the elevator and ask what are the five most important things the company is working on for the next six months, that person should be able to tell you, rapid fire, one, two, three, four, five, ideally using the same words you've used in your communications to the staff and, if they're really good, in the same order. If not, the heartbeat isn't strong enough yet.

IN BRIEF

▶ Employees at all levels want and need to understand not only the particular work they are assigned and their team's mission, but also the larger story of the way the business works, the challenges the company faces, and the competitive landscape.

▶ Truly understanding how the business works is the most valuable learning, more productive and appealing than "employee development" trainings. It's the rocket fuel of high performance and lifelong learning.

▶ Communication between management and employees should genuinely flow both ways. The more leaders encourage questions and suggestions and make themselves accessible for give-and-take, the more employees at all levels will offer ideas and insights that will amaze you.

▶ If someone working for you seems clueless, chances are they have not been told information they need to know. Make sure you haven't failed to give it to them.

▶ If you don't tell your people about how the business is doing and the problems being confronted—good, bad, and ugly—then they will get that information somewhere else, and it will often be misinformation.

▶ The job of communicating is never done. It's not an annual or quarterly or even monthly or weekly function. A steady stream of communication is the lifeblood of competitive advantage.

QUESTIONS TO CONSIDER

- How well do you think people throughout the company could describe its business model? Why not ask them to do so? No prompts allowed.

- Do you share with employees the same information presented in your company's earnings calls? How frequently do you show them the company's P&L? Where are they likely to get data about how your company stacks up against the competition?

- Is everyone aware of difficult challenges your company faces? Have you asked them their thoughts about how to tackle these? Do you have a disciplined process for disseminating information and discussing challenges?

- What areas of your business do you think your people know little to nothing about? Could you ask a leader in that domain to come and talk to your team? Are there any other ways you could facilitate communication between the groups?

- How well do you think your people understand who the customer is and what their needs and desires are? Do you regularly share customer research? Can you facilitate your team spending some time with customers?

- If you were going to hold an off-site, what is the most pressing issue you would want your people to learn about and debate? How could you provide the richest possible presentation of information?

- What existing meetings or forums could be used to carve out dedicated time for communicating more about the business context? Do you regularly review these meetings to be sure they still are effective? Do you set different agendas for different kinds of communication (for example, a weekly stand-up versus a quarterly all-hands meeting)?

CHAPTER THREE

Humans Hate Being Lied To
and Being Spun

| *Practice Radical Honesty* |

One of the most important insights anyone in business can have is that it's not cruel to tell people the truth respectfully and honestly. To the contrary, being transparent and telling people what they need to hear is the only way to ensure they both trust you and understand you.

Most of us feel that we can't tell the people who work for us or with us the truth because (a) they're not smart enough to understand it, (b) they're not mature enough to understand it, or (c) it wouldn't be nice. What's so wrong with this? After all, humans want to be nice. We want to treat one another well, and we think that means making one another feel good.

But this desire to make people feel good is often as much a desire to make ourselves feel good as to do the right thing. It often leads to people actually feeling worse, because they're not correcting a problem in the way they're working, and that eventually comes home to roost.

Part of being an adult is being able hear the truth. And the corollary is that you owe the adults you hire the truth. That is actually what they want most from you.

Have You Said This to Their Face?

One of the most important mandates at Netflix was that people talk openly about issues with one another. That went for subordinates, colleagues, and bosses. We wanted honesty to flow up and down, all around the company.

A big part of why Reed Hastings and I worked so well together is that we've always been so honest with each other. Reed liked how honest I was not only with him but with everyone at the company. When I told one of my old HR colleagues, who had heard lots of my stories about working with Reed at Pure Software, that I was going over to Netflix, she said, "What?! You're going to another start-up with the Animal?" I had forgotten I'd sometimes called him that. He could be really tough in those days. But he expected a lot from me and I was always challenged to deliver.

Practicing radical honesty is like breathing to me, which didn't always put me in good graces at other companies. One reason I decided to move from the corporate world to the start-up world when I went to work for Reed at Pure was that I was always getting in trouble. I'd be called to the VP of HR's office, and he'd ask, "Did you make fun of the engineers?" And I'd say, "Yes, but seriously! They're complaining that the hot tubs were not hot enough, the towels aren't fluffy enough, and the pool is too cold." And he'd reprimand me, "You know our engineers are our most important resource and you have to give them special treatment!" I just wasn't buying that. As I said before, I'd gotten quite tired of their being treated like gods.

With Reed, things couldn't have been more different. When I interviewed with him, one of his first questions was "What's your HR philosophy?" Remember, I'd worked at Sun and at Borland, so I answered in my fluent HR-speak: "Reed, I believe that everyone should draw a line from their personal ambitions and integrity and become empowered to contribute." He looked at me and said, "Do you even speak English? You know what you just said didn't mean anything, right? Those words don't even string together into a logical sentence!"

I responded with characteristic aplomb, "Hey, you don't even know me!"

He shot right back, "How am I supposed to know you when we're having this kind of conversation? Tell me, what would you do that would make my company grow?"

When I got home that day and my husband asked me how the interviews had gone, I told him, "Well, I got into a fight with the CEO." Fortunately, I got the job, and I quickly came to love how blunt Reed and I could be with each other. He always challenged my assumptions and called out any HR truisms I might spout, and that felt great. I felt respected. Reed never coddled me in the slightest, and I loved the way he pushed me to keep finding new ways to improve the business. As soon as I had accomplished something I was really proud of, he would say, "Okay, that was great! So now what?"

One of the pillars of the Netflix culture was that if people had a problem with an employee or with how a colleague in their own department or somewhere else in the company was doing something, they were expected to talk about it openly with that person, ideally face to face. We didn't want any criticizing behind people's backs. Because I was the head of HR, managers would often complain to me about an employee or someone in another department. I'd always say, "Have you told her yet?"

Holding people to this standard of transparency has many benefits. One is that it puts the clamp on politicking and backstabbing. I've often said that I hate company politics, not just because it's nasty but because it's so inefficient. Think about it. If I'm going to stab someone in the back, I have to go get a knife, hide it, wait until I'm alone with that person, and catch them off guard. I'd better be sure to kill them or they'll come back after me. It takes planning, and it's high risk. Wouldn't it be a whole lot easier just to tell that person, "It makes me crazy when you do that, so please stop!" More important, though, is that honesty helps people to grow, and it flushes out the differences of opinion and alternative ideas that people so often keep to themselves.

People Learn to Welcome Criticism

Openly sharing criticism was one of the hardest parts of the Netflix culture for new employees to get used to, but most quickly came to appreciate how valuable the openness was. When I talked about this with one of our great team leaders, Eric Colson, he told me the giving and taking of honest feedback was central to how well his teams worked, and his teams worked beautifully. That's why Eric rose to the position of VP of data science and engineering in less than three years at the company, having begun as an individual contributor. He'd been managing a small data analytics team at Yahoo! before coming to Netflix, and he recalled that the culture there was to be super supportive of people and not to criticize them. He told me that when he started getting critical feedback from colleagues at Netflix, "It hurt. People told me, 'Colson, you're not good with communication; when you need to get a message out to a wide audience, you take too long to make the point and it's unclear.'" His initial reaction was to think, *Oh yeah? Well, I've got a lot of things to say about you too!* But before long, he realized that "when you reflect on what they've said, you see it from their point of view, and you learn how to improve on those things. That directness was really helpful." Again and again at Netflix I saw that people rebounded quickly from the initial shock of receiving negative feedback and learned not only to appreciate it but to deliver it themselves much more consistently and thoughtfully.

Eric also shared with me a story that reinforced what I observed so often when managers weren't willing to give their people tough feedback: that it puts undue pressure on the boss to provide cover and cheats the employee of the chance to improve. He recalled having held back a badly needed critique from one of his staff at Yahoo! and then having to make up for that person's shortfalls, which was exhausting—and unfair to the employee. "I was too kind," he told me, "and that means you're a bad manager in a lot of ways. You end up sugarcoating things, and that's doing them a disservice."

Practice Your Delivery

We worked hard at Netflix to engender the kind of belief Eric expresses in the value of totally honest feedback, and to coach managers so that they felt comfortable delivering it. That was a major focus of my time. Sometimes I would just let the person with the issue vent, loudly and passionately. They'd recite in detail all the bad behavior of the person they were annoyed with. Then I would ask, "What did she say when you told her that?" Typically, the person complaining would say, "I can't say this to her!" I'd push back, "But you said it to me, didn't you?" and they'd look sheepish, realizing it wasn't right to unload behind the person's back. Then we would practice the same conversation without the emotion. We'd also discuss the importance of giving specific examples of the problematic behavior and proposing solutions. Following those rules makes such conversations actually constructive.

Practice is crucial for honing your delivery style. You can do it in front of a mirror or with your spouse or a friend. Actually rehearsing what you'll say, out loud, allows you to hear the tone of your voice. You might even want to record yourself. It's also important to think about your body language, which can speak louder than words. We're often totally unaware of how emphatically it's sending a negative message. A friend told me that when she went for coaching about how to talk to her boss—who was so difficult that her whole team had trouble communicating with her—the coach had my friend do some role play showing how she typically talked to her boss. The coach exclaimed, "Well, I'm sure she knows how annoyed you are with her!" My friend's hand gestures had spoken volumes. The coach told her to sit on her hands during meetings with her boss, and that dramatically improved their conversations.

The most important thing about giving feedback is that it must be about behavior, rather than some essentializing characterization of a person, like "You're unfocused." It also must be actionable. The person receiving it has to understand the specific changes in their actions that are being requested. The comment "You're making a great effort, but you're not getting enough done" is essentially meaningless. An action version would be "I can see how hard you're working, and I really appreciate that, but I've noticed that there are some things you're spending too much time on at the expense of others that are more important." You would then establish a better prioritization with the person. I once received an extraordinarily helpful piece of feedback that is a model for being direct and suggesting the solution. Someone who worked closely with me and was often with me in meetings told me that I should talk less. "You're always talking so much that others don't get a chance to get their two cents in." Done. I started to catch myself and make sure that I shut up and listened more.

Many people feel hesitant to speak so openly, but the truth is that most people really appreciate the opportunity to get a better understanding of their behavior and how it's being perceived, as long as the tone of delivery isn't hostile or condescending.

Model Honesty and People Will Pick the Habit Up

You want everyone on your team—and, for upper management, all around the company—to learn to be more open and honest with one another. For this to happen, the standard must be set and practiced from the top down. The Netflix executive team modeled honesty in a number of ways. One was to conduct an exercise we called "Start, Stop, Continue" in our team meetings. In this drill, each person tells a colleague one thing they should start doing, one thing they should stop doing, and one thing they're doing really well and should keep doing. We were such believers in the value of transparency that we did this exercise in our meetings, out loud in front of the group. Recognition of how important it is to be open rippled down through the company as we'd go back to our teams and report that the executive team had just done "Start, Stop, Continue" and fill them in on what had been said. That wasn't a mandate; I didn't make it an HR initiative. Most of the executives just did it, which exemplifies the power of modeling. A few told me it would never work with their teams, and I'd say to them, "Well, you know, they're doing it in product and in marketing, and it seems to be working there because they're getting lots of great work done." That was usually quite compelling.

We also modeled radical honesty from the top down by requiring it of all our team leaders in managing their people and coaching them on how to provide it. We insisted that they share feedback on a continual basis. In addition, we asked them to explicitly set the standard with their teams that it was unacceptable to talk about people behind their backs or to come to them to complain about a colleague, unless, of course, the problem was one concerning ethical violations, such as sexual harassment, which was treated with confidentiality.

Another one of our great team builders was Rochelle King, who started out managing a small design team and became the manager of a large group as VP of user experience and product services. She recalled that it was difficult at first for her to give such open, honest feedback, but that because it was such a strong mandate, she realized she had no choice but to get comfortable with it. She said, "I felt as a leader that I would have to do the hard things in order to uphold the culture, things that were against my nature, such as having the difficult conversations to people's faces. I knew that was something I had to abide by, the completely uncomfortable act of going and talking to someone about a problem. When

it's so much a part of the culture, you hold yourself accountable to it. There were lots of stories of other leaders doing it,
and so you did it too."

The more rigorously you communicate and model the
transparency standard, the more pervasive a part of your culture it will become.

Provide Mechanisms for Feedback

Eventually we decided we wanted to facilitate the offering of
critiques not only to one's direct reports and teammates but
to colleagues all around the company. So we created a system
for sending "Start, Stop, Continue" feedback to anyone at the
company once a year. We picked an annual feedback day and
asked that everybody send their comments, in "Start, Stop,
Continue" format, to everyone they had feedback for. This
is a great example of how the practices we used to create the
culture evolved as we tried new things. At first we made the
system anonymous. But, true to form, the engineers rebelled.
Management was saying people should be open and honest,
yet the tool we had provided lacked transparency. They simply started to sign their names to their critiques within the
message text. The executive team realized they had a good
point, and we revised the system.

To make sure that people understood we truly didn't
want them to hold back, I monitored how actively people
were entering critiques. I didn't want them to write just a few
bits of softball criticism to a couple of team members they
knew well. The whole point was that we were providing a
platform for widespread transparency. Eric Colson told me
that the first time he had to write his feedback he thought,
If I've only written comments for a few people, I'm going to

hear from Patty, "What's this? You work with fifty people and you only gave feedback to three of them?!" If you institute a process like this, you will probably have to hold people accountable to step up and avidly participate.

There's no question that this process took some getting used to. Eric described how anxious he was the first time through. "I didn't like the way a product manager was doing a certain thing," he said, "and I remember hovering over that submit button, thinking, *Oh God, what's he going to think of me? Is this going to piss him off?* But the next day when everybody got their feedback, to my surprise, he came by my desk and said, 'Hey, I got your feedback; thank you, that was very helpful.'" Eric recalled that he came to really look forward to feedback-sharing day. In my experience, probably 90 percent of people reacted that way, and often the feedback would lead to productive conversations that really helped clear the air.

Everyone Deserves to Know About Problems with the Business Too

We practiced this same radical honesty about the challenges the business was facing. It was a very bumpy ride in the early years, and we shared with the whole company the difficulties as we encountered them, being very clear about our time frame, our metrics, and what it would take to meet goals. We wanted to make sure all of our people understood where we were going and what we were doing, and I realized that an essential part of that was understanding, really deeply understanding, what the business was up against. In most companies, no one owns the responsibility of communicating this information company-wide, and too often many people—whole departments, even—are left in the dark. Companies sometimes even delay making important strategy and operations changes because of worry about how employees will react.

At Netflix we learned that preparing people for changes to come led to a sense of trust around the company: trust that we would proactively take the company where it needed to go and that we wouldn't mislead anyone about the changes that would require. For sure, sometimes those changes weren't popular. One of our big early challenges was making the transition to streaming. We had always talked about video streaming as the future of our business, and we tracked the habits of our customers very closely as we got better at delivery and built up our content. During that time, we had many open, heated debates about what the transition would mean to our customers. Transparency about the difficulty of the decisions didn't make coming to them any easier, but the honest dialogue did mean that people all over the company were prepared. It also meant that we made the right decisions at the right times. We didn't delay out of worry about a shock to the system for employees. Sure, the transition was tough, and some people weren't happy, but there was no lack of clarity about what to expect.

Too often upper management thinks that sharing about problems confronting the business will heighten anxiety among staff, but what's much more anxiety provoking is not knowing. You can't protect your people from hard truths anyway. And holding back the truth, or telling them half-truths, will only breed contempt. Trust is based on honest communication, and I find that employees become cynical when they hear half-truths. Cynicism is a cancer. It creates a metastasizing discontent that feeds on itself, leading to smarminess and fueling backstabbing.

Admit When You're Wrong and You'll Get Better Input

Somebody asked me once, "What would you fire me for?" I said, "That's a good question. Let me think. Well, certainly embezzlement, sexual harassment, or breach of confidentiality. Wait, I know what I'd fire you for. If we were discussing something that went wrong, doing a postmortem, and you said, 'Oh, I knew that was a problem but nobody asked me.' Then I'd probably run you over in the parking lot, because you would allow something to go wrong that you saw was coming."

The other vital point about honesty concerning business issues is that it's got to go both ways. Employees should be told never to withhold questions or information from you or their direct superiors. As a leader, you should model this, showing, not just telling, that you want people to speak up and that you can be told bad news directly and disagreed with. Otherwise most people will never be truly open with you. A study by Deloitte showed that 70 percent of employees in a wide range of sectors "admit to remaining silent about issues that might compromise performance."

Say you're in a meeting and are about to make a decision. One of your direct reports at the table has been bending your ear for months about what a stupid idea he thinks it is. Yet here you are at the end of the meeting and that person hasn't spoken up. You should call that out. Say, "You know, we're about to make a decision that you've been telling me for four months you're against, and you haven't said a word. Have you changed your mind? Or do you feel like I'm not going to listen?" You have to exhibit the courage you want people to have, the courage to say, "I honestly don't think that's a good idea at all, and here's why."

Of course, it's one thing to get honest input from colleagues on your own level, or from your boss, and another to get it from your subordinates. But that is exactly what you want. Because you are absolutely not always going to be right, and the satisfaction of being right can be very dangerous. I was a huge fan of that satisfaction. I used to love being right. When I had told Reed or another executive I thought something they had decided to do was a bad idea and I turned out to be right, I took great pleasure in that. One time Reed sent me an email saying, "You were right, I was wrong," and I printed it out and kept it in my wallet. I only got those about every three years, so they were a big deal to me! But then one day we were talking about something and he said, "You were right. I was wrong about this one," and it didn't feel good anymore. Instead I was mad at myself because I hadn't made my case more effectively earlier. I found myself wondering how I could have made a better argument.

When leaders not only are open to being wrong but also readily admit it—as Reed did that day, and regularly did—and when they do so publicly, they send a powerful message to their teams: *Please speak up!*

One of the best ways to get all the cards on the table is to help people see that those who speak up live to see another day. Reed was great at this. I love the story Tom Willerer told me about a time he disagreed with Reed in a team meeting of about thirty-five people. Facebook had started doing frictionless sharing in the Newsfeed about what people were posting, such as what they were reading or watching and events they were going to. Reed was intent on Netflix getting on this bandwagon and having information about what members were watching feed directly to their Facebook pages. Tom thought members should be given the option to select which information would be shared, and Reed passionately disagreed. The two debated the point vigorously in front of the group. Tom pressed the point that survey data showed that members wanted the choice, and Reed agreed to let Tom and his team perform an A/B test to see which approach was better. When the data showed that Tom was right, Reed openly announced to that same group, "Look, I debated hard against this, but Tom was right. Great job."

Tom took the wisdom of modeling how to be wrong to his role as chief product officer at Coursera. He delightedly told me how wrong he had been about a big idea he brought to the company. Arriving with his "bright, shiny Netflix background," he was sure that Coursera should start streaming its classes 24/7, so that people could start a course whenever they wanted. The professors teaching the classes argued that courses should be offered only at the starts of semesters, just as in brick-and-mortar colleges. They said students needed a hard start of that kind and deadlines to motivate them to keep up. Tom thought that approach was outmoded and pressed ahead with streaming a number of classes, designing a fancy new interface as well. What happened? Many more people started those classes, but many fewer finished them. That was a big problem for Coursera. The business model is not just about offering lots of classes; it's about people actually learning and getting credits. The professors were right that hard deadlines are important for learning. But Tom wasn't completely wrong. Ultimately, through more testing, the company came up with a blended model in which courses start every two weeks; there are due dates for assignments, but students know that if they fall behind, they can start again in just two weeks.

That is exactly the kind of honest debate and disagreement from below that is smothered at so many companies. This may be why a study by the Corporate Executive Board found that companies that actively fostered honest feedback and had more open communication produced a return over a ten-year period that was an astonishing 270 percent higher than that of companies that didn't.

When People Share Openly, It's Harder to Rewrite History

Transparency also helps ensure that people take ownership of the positions they've advocated and don't get hopelessly caught up in finger-pointing after the fact, or at least not as much. Let's face it: it's fun to say "I told you so." But it's toxic to productive problem solving.

One of the most difficult failures we had at Netflix was our decision to divide our business into a DVD rental service (which we called Qwikster) and a streaming service (which kept the Netflix name), and to increase our subscription rates for each at the same time. It was a train wreck. Customers were outraged, and within about a month we reversed course, issuing a public apology. I'm not going to claim that there were no recriminations or calls of "I told you so." But the fact was that the executive team had agreed on the strategy and everyone had had the chance to object. Rochelle King, who by then had been promoted to the executive team, recalled when I talked about this with her, "What was interesting was the way the company acted in the aftermath, doing a great job of pulling together, getting all of the VPs across all functions to think through what they were going to do. We were all fully aware of the strategy. Due to the culture of transparency, the whole team had to take responsibility for what happened."

Anonymous Surveys Send a Mixed Message

The engineers who rebelled against our anonymous feedback system did so out of a depth of respect for the value of open, attributed contributions. This is one of the things I love about engineers. When they write code, every little bit of their handiwork is clearly identified as theirs, and they've learned that being able to trace errors, as well as great pieces of coding, to individuals helps everyone write better programs. They were right to push for the change to our feedback system. Once the sources of comments were identified, feedback became more thoughtful and productive.

The conventional thinking is that if you allow people to be anonymous, they will be more truthful. In my experience that's not the case. Truthful people are truthful in everything they do. And if you don't know who is giving you feedback, how can you put their comments into the context of the work they're doing, who their manager is, and what kind of employee they are? Perhaps the worst problem with anonymous surveys, though, is that they send the message that it's best to be most honest when people don't know who you are.

I was talking to an HR director recently who told me she'd just gotten the results of her company's semiannual employee survey and wanted to discuss some HR initiatives she was planning to roll out as a result. I asked her if the company had hired an outside firm to do an anonymous engagement survey. She said yes, that she had talked the management into spending the money because she knew how important it was. I asked her who came up with the questions. She said they'd picked one of the software programs that are available for purchase off the shelf. I said, "I betcha someone complained that you took away the four kinds of flavored water in the fridge, right?" My point was that if you rely on anonymous surveys and prescribed questions, you will not get quality information. If you want to know what people are thinking, there is no good replacement for simply asking them, best of all face to face. That company consisted of seventy employees. They should have simply broken people into seven groups of ten and asked people to share their thoughts.

Your people can handle the truth, straight and in person, and so can you.

IN BRIEF

▶ People can handle being told the truth, about both the business and their performance. The truth is not only what they need but also what they intensely want.

▶ Telling the truth about perceived problems, in a timely fashion and face to face, is the single most effective way to solve problems.

▶ Practicing radical honesty diffuses tensions and discourages backstabbing; it builds understanding and respect.

▶ Radical honesty also leads to the sharing of opposing views, which are so often withheld and which can lead to vital insights.

▶ Failing to tell people the truth about problems in their performance leads to an undue burden being shouldered by managers and other team members.

▶ The style of delivery is important; leaders should practice giving critical feedback so that it is specific and constructive and comes across as well intentioned.

► Consider setting up a system for colleagues to offer one another critiques. We created a successful one at Netflix and instituted an annual feedback day for the whole company to share comments with anyone they had thoughts for.

► Model openly admitting when you are wrong. In addition, talk about what went into your decisions and where you went wrong. That encourages employees to share ideas and opposing views with you, even if they directly contradict your position.

QUESTIONS TO CONSIDER

- How open have you been with your team about the current prospects of your business and the most difficult problems the company and your team are dealing with? Do people at all levels know the challenges the company is facing in the next six months?

- Are people free to disagree with a point made by someone in authority during a team meeting? Have they seen it done openly, in front of the whole team?

- Are there team members who rarely, if ever, speak up with ideas and concerns? Have you called on them or spoken with them about contributing?

- When was the last time you talked openly with your team about a mistake you made in addressing a business issue?

- Is there someone on your team who is underperforming but with whom you haven't seriously discussed the problem? What impact do you think that person's performance issues have on the rest of the team?

- When you do discuss performance issues with people, do you generally feel that they have understood the specific problems with how they're doing their work?

- How valuable do you think it would be for your team to receive feedback from people in other areas of the company? Is there any way you can facilitate such cross-functional sharing?

CHAPTER FOUR

Debate Vigorously

*| Cultivate Strong Opinions and Argue
About Them Only on the Facts |*

Our Netflix executive team was fierce. We were combative in that beautiful, intellectual way where you argue to tease out someone's viewpoint, because although you don't agree, you think the other person is really smart so you want to understand why they think what they think. That respect for one another's intelligence and genuine desire to discover the bases of colleagues' views drove intense mutual questioning and kept it mostly productive and civil, if often quite colorful. The team also modeled this vigorous questioning for employees in many forums, openly debating one another.

Probably the main reason the company could continually reinvent itself and thrive, despite so many truly daunting challenges coming at us so fast and furiously, was that we taught people to ask, "How do you know that's true?" Or my favorite variant, "Can you help me understand what leads you to believe that's true?" For example, we had a terrible struggle to decrease buffering time (the amount of time between clicking on a video and it starting). It was a beastly problem that only the engineers could really understand. We told our sales and marketing people that it was not okay to vent to the engineers, "You have to fix the god****ed buffering problem!" They should ask, "Help me understand why buffering takes so long." And we made it very clear that the question ought to be asked genuinely. If people ask in a true spirit of interest about the problems others are wrestling with, remarkable bridges of understanding can be built. The answer to the buffering question was extremely eye-opening to the nontechnical staff, who had no idea what a daunting challenge the engineers were up against.

Over time, this sort of questioning helped cultivate curiosity and respect and led to invaluable learning both within and among teams and functions. It also prevented all sorts of rumormongering and back-channel communication. I was so proud the day I heard an engineer say to a marketing manager, with obvious sincerity, "I hear you spent $7 million to acquire customers. Can you tell me how that worked?"

This practice often took some time for newly hired managers to get used to. One guy with a big résumé introduced himself to his team by calling an all-hands meeting, which I decided to attend. When he started lecturing them about a problem they had been working furiously on, one of the engineers raised his hand and said, "We're so excited to have you here and we can't wait to learn from you, but I think you should know that we're aware of this problem and we've been working really hard on it." The new guy hadn't bothered to discover that the team had in fact made phenomenal progress on it. As I walked out of the meeting with the new manager, he turned to me and said, "Who does that guy think he is? How dare he talk to me that way!" I told him that the engineer was one of our best, and that we had cultivated the practice of asking people about the nature of problems they were tackling rather than assuming an understanding of them. Netflix turned out to be too much of a culture change for him, and he moved on before long.

Much more common was that people learned to appreciate the ethic of asking.

Have an Opinion, and Be Right Most of the Time

There is no problem with people having strong opinions. On the contrary, it's important that they do and that they argue for them vigorously. However, people's opinions should always be fact based. Insisting that decision making be fact driven doesn't detract from the importance of opinions. It just means people are expected to try really hard to make sure theirs are well founded. I often say to executives, "Have an opinion; take a stand; be right most of the time." Opinions aren't helpful unless the people who hold them are willing to take a stand in their defense by making a fact-based case. One of the great dangers in business is people who are great at winning an argument due to their powers of persuasion rather than the merits of their case. We had one guy who was just fantastic at championing his views. I mean, you'd listen to him and you'd just about be in a trance; he was so eloquent and so convincing. But he was almost always wrong.

We set a standard at Netflix that people should develop their opinions by probing into facts and by listening with an open mind to fact-based arguments they didn't agree with. This flowed naturally from the fact that most of the early employees were mathematicians and engineers. They lived and breathed the scientific method, which is all about discovering facts and then adjusting one's understanding of the problem and the way to solve it. As the company grew, we consciously cultivated that obsession with being fact driven and scientific—all around the company, not just in engineering. You don't need a company founded on engineering in order to widely instill this ethic.

Note that I say "fact driven," not "data driven." There's been something of a deification of data in recent years, as though data itself is the answer, the ultimate truth. There's a dangerous fallacy that data constitutes the facts you need to know to run your business. Hard data is absolutely vital, of course, but you also need qualitative insight and well-formulated opinions, and you need your team to debate those insights and opinions openly and with gusto.

Data Doesn't Have an Opinion

I loved when we hired somebody new in data science, especially in the early days. We all had our own beliefs about customer behavior that they'd bust. In the beginning we opined about how the customer behaved based on ourselves as customers. We would argue back and forth, saying, "That's not the way they watch; no, no, I don't watch that way." Then with the transition to streaming, we started to get actual viewing data. Before that we'd only known which DVDs we shipped to people and which they put in their queues (the now all-but-forgotten feature allowing people to line up as many items as they wanted, to be sent to them as soon as the DVDs were back in stock. Now all of a sudden we could see which content was actually watched most avidly. Who knew people were so crazy about shows like *Storage Wars* and *Swamp People*? The rush of data dispelled many of our old myths.

Data is great; data is powerful. I love data. But the problem is that people become overly wedded to data and too often consider it much too narrowly, removed from the wider business context. They consider it the answer to rather than the basis of good questions. I love a distinction Ted Sarandos made to me about how data is best used. He said the decision making of his content team was data informed rather than data driven. When Netflix launched *House of Cards*, lots of attention was given to how Ted's team had done such a deft job of mining Netflix viewership data: they concluded the show would be a good fit in part because because the show's star was popular with viewers, as was another drama set in the halls of Washington power, *The West Wing*. In reality, while the data gave a great assist, a huge part of the decision to go with the show was that the remarkably talented David Fincher was developing it.

Ted stresses that insights from data analysis complement his team's decision making but certainly don't dictate it. They've seen that a project can fail even with all sorts of supporting data. Whether to move forward with a show or film is very much a judgment call. When the team decided to go ahead with *Orange Is the New Black*, they overrode their mandate that shows had to have well-developed scripts, not because data was telling them the show would be a hit but because of the vision of the show's creator, Jenji Kohan, which was brilliantly thought out. The show is based on a book, and others had wanted to develop it for the screen, but there were worries that viewers wouldn't be sympathetic to the prisoners and that a prison might be a claustrophobic setting. Kohan planned to expand the storytelling to take viewers into the inmates' lives before they were sent to prison. Doing so would show that so many of the women who end up in such low-security prisons, as the author of the book did, are far from hardened criminals, making them more sympathetic and engaging viewers in their life stories.

The content team has been regularly surprised by responses to original programming, with some shows being much stronger draws than expected and others the reverse. They take that viewer-response data not as an end point in deciding how to proceed with a show but as a launching point for interrogating their understanding of the response. If a show falls flat, they ask whether that was due to a creative failing or was a matter of marketing or positioning. Ted also pointed out that viewership data can be limited in its ability to provide information about what people would *like* to watch if they *could*. When Netflix began planning to go global, the conventional wisdom about what international viewers wanted to watch was skewed by global box office data. The data seemed to suggest that overseas viewers weren't all that interested in a number of American shows. What that data couldn't factor in was that people in many countries had very limited access to American programming. When Netflix made so much of that programming available for the first time, across the board, people flocked to it. Ted said of his team's content-creation process, "There is lots of intuition that is acted on, and I look for people for the team who are smart enough to read the data and intuitive enough to know how to ignore it."

Ted also cautions that data can be used as an accountability shield, deflecting responsibility for a judgment call. People are more comfortable making decisions based on hard data in part because they can fall back on that data if the decision turns out to be wrong. Television series pilots are a great case in point. Because they are tested with viewers, if a show ultimately fails, the production team can always say, "Well, it tested really well." Ted's team hasn't followed the pilot model; they green-light production of a whole season all at once.

People can also be biased about which data they marshal. And we've all seen that people tend to privilege their own data over that of others. Marketing hauls out one set of data and sales another. Data is only one component of problem solving. Even if everyone, across all teams, has all the same data, you need people to challenge one another about aspects of the business that no spreadsheet can speak to.

Beware of Data That Looks Great but Doesn't Matter

Because software engineers know I like them, they constantly approach me to take a look at their new products. One wanted me to review his fancy new HR management software. He completely filled the whiteboard with the product map of the software, an elaborate system waterfalling goals down from upper management to individual contributors. All that data was entered into the software, and then there was an extraordinarily intense employee assessment that took two hours, with a facilitator for each individual, in order to populate all the data fields for a giant relational database. I stopped him and said, "Can I say something? Can I stop you right there? So I need to hire somebody from your firm to sit down with each of my employees for two hours to fill out this form"—it was online, but it was essentially a form—"and with the roll-up of all these goals, it's

going to spit out an algorithm and it's going to give me what?"
He said, "Well, HR will finally have data." So I asked him,
"What will they do with this data?" And he answered, "Well,
they'll finally have it!" Can I just say, *What??!* Why should anyone spend so much time and money just to create data?

One of the biggest mistakes is fixating on metrics that
don't matter. Take HR and its obsession with retention. HR is
the department that is supposed to take care of people's well-be-
ing, and supposedly the key metric to measure that is retention,
yet 50 percent of what HR does is say good-bye to people.

I was consulting to an executive team recently, and
their head of HR told me that they're concerned about keeping people because everyone will leave for a better perk or
more money. I asked, "How do you know that's true?" In
my experience, the best people are not swayed by perks. But
I also question whether turnover is really such a big problem. It depends on the context. If you're working on a project
that's a heads-down three- or four-year job that requires a
lot of people putting in a lot of effort, and the training and
assimilation cycle is very long, then you definitely want people
to stay engaged for that time. But even so, the way to keep
employees committed is to hire people who are really interested in a problem like the one you're hiring for and who have
a track record of or proclivity for working on things for a very
long time. It's not to offer them four kinds of flavored water
and sleeping pods. Often companies have much shorter-term
needs, and when a task has been completed, it's best for both
the company and the employees if you tell them it's time to
look for a new job. About which more later.

Another big mistake made with metrics is thinking that
they're fixed. They must be fluid; they must be continuously
revisited and questioned. This is where vigorous debate comes in.

Debate Only for the Sake of the Business and Customers

While our debates at Netflix often got heated, they generally didn't become mean-spirited or counterproductive, because we set a standard that they should all essentially be about serving the business and our customers.

One of the worst ways that companies fail to serve their customers, and therefore their own profitability, is neglecting to interrogate intensively enough what the data is really telling them. Often a business must choose between two alternatives for catering to customer needs and preferences, both of which have strong data-backed arguments behind them. Making these calls requires judgment to complement the data. A great mechanism we created for keeping the focus on customers and ensuring that we rigorously and openly debated such difficult judgment calls was a monthly forum, the Consumer Science Meeting. The name was a riff on computer science, a way of saying that while we were absolutely an innovator of data-intensive analytics, our computing was all in the service of pleasing customers. Reed and our heads of marketing and product always attended, and members of the content team often came up from LA. I almost always went because it was a fantastically informative meeting that kept me up to speed with the leading edge of business development.

The purpose of the meeting was to present the results of all the consumer tests we'd done the previous month and the arguments for those planned for the current month. The employees who had devised and run the tests made the presentations, and the executives' role was to intensively question them about the results and their rationales for the upcoming tests. One of those often in the hot seat was Steve McLendon, who had started at the company in print marketing and been promoted into many roles in the marketing group that involved testing. Ultimately he had moved over to the product group as director of product innovation, an extraordinary accomplishment. Steve is quick to say that he was something of a fish out of water when he joined Netflix. He had no prior experience with anything like the intensity of our business. He had been selling ad space for a small print periodical in Santa Cruz, and he was originally in charge of placing our print ads, a positively archaic business compared with the booming frontier of online targeting. Steve is also a naturally laid-back guy. I was curious to hear his reflections on facing the barrage of questioning in the Consumer Science Meeting, and he made no bones about how stressful it could be. But his main point was that "you learn how to come in and think about things in a structured way, anticipate the kind of questions you're going to get, and have your argument as buttoned up as you can." He said that because both marketing and product heads were present, he also learned to think much better from both perspectives.

Every intense disagreement we had about serving customers better found its way into the Consumer Science Meeting. Our debates there underscored that no one, no matter how experienced or high level, could fully understand customer needs and desires purely on the basis of their experience or brilliance. We often went into tests with sharp divisions in our expectations about the results. One of the most heated of these concerned the queue feature. Our data clearly showed that customers *loved* the queue. It was a big brand builder and driver of customer loyalty. But once we moved to streaming, we no longer needed the queue; everyone who wanted to could stream the same content all at once. Should we do away with the beloved queue? Views were strongly divided.

We took the debate to the data. Customer surveys showed

that a relatively small segment were adamantly opposed to doing away with the queue. But A/B tests showed that it made no material difference in customer retention or the number of movies or shows watched or any of the other hard-data measures of customer satisfaction. We decided to do away with it, because doing so would free up system capability for enhancing the quality of our streaming. After some initial vocal protest from the minority of ardent fans, the change was embraced.

Steve McLendon reminded me of another such counter-intuitive test result, this one about the customer sign-up process. The findings floored him. We were constantly running tests on the process, but this was a particularly controversial one. The hypothesis was that we could boost the number of people who signed up for a free trial, and then ultimately subscribed, if we removed friction from the initial sign-up by not requiring people to input their credit card information. Steve was adamant that subscriptions would dramatically increase, yet the results were abysmal: they plummeted *by half*. He was so stunned that he really wanted to run the test again. Debating the result, we realized that, ironically, in trying to remove friction we had introduced *more* by effectively forcing people to go through a sign-up process twice.

Earn a Reputation for Selflessness

Executives tell me all the time about virtual wars raging between department heads. They can't conceive of the possibility of conducting open debate about core business issues without its escalating into counterproductive dispute, even internecine battle. Well, it's true that if you and I disagree on something and have a knock-down, drag-out fight about it, and I think you're fighting for your ego or department or pet idea, then I'm going think of a clever way to get around you. But if I believe that you're fighting for the good of the company, defined as doing the right thing for the customer, then I'll be more willing to hear you. In the Consumer Science Meeting, as is human nature, often enough people would go off on a tear, slipping into argument for argument's sake, but someone would always interject, "And how does this help the customer exactly?" Diversion averted.

Another way of establishing that you are being selfless in your advocacy is to avidly recognize the problem-solving contributions of others. Reed, again, modeled this well. John Ciancutti recalled a particularly telling case. One of the reasons we needed the queue in the DVD days was that managing the inventory and getting discs to customers quickly was an incredibly difficult task. We had millions of movies coming in and out each day; we were shipping more items than Amazon was—and, of course, we had to create the capacity not only to ship them out but to get them back and then ship them out quickly again. A particular problem was that certain titles tended to disproportionately accumulate at different distribution centers, and John proposed an idea for a way to solve that problem. "I had a theory of why the accumulations were happening," he recalled, "and I pushed it a couple different times and didn't get pickup on it. We tried everything else, and then in a meeting a long time later, Reed threw up his hands in desperation and said, 'Well, let's try Ciancutti's idea.' I looked up and said, 'What idea?' I had actually forgotten about it, but Reed had remembered." The team tried it out, and it worked. Reed had listened carefully enough to John's idea that he had internalized it and could actually recall it after its originator had forgotten about it. As John said, "That's the kind of respect he would give you. He was listening to this idea that nobody thought was a good one."

That story also highlights that even with avid, selfless debate, good ideas will sometimes get shot down. Which is another reason it's so important that people recognize that even the most compelling, fact-based arguments can be wrong, and that "fact-based" does not equal "true." It also underscores the importance of revisiting conclusions. Quite often conclusions we thought we'd debated to death had to be revisited and debated all over again.

Orchestrate the Debates You Want

At one point a big disagreement arose between Netflix's head of marketing and head of content concerning how we thought about our customers. It was developing into a real tussle, because both executives were very strong-minded, and both had good reasons for their views. Reed did a beautiful thing. He arranged a debate between the two, onstage, in chairs facing each other, in front of the rest of the executive team. And the really brilliant twist was that each one argued the other's side. To prep for that, they really had to get into the other person's skin.

Reed made this style of formal debate a regular practice for the product development team. Once a month he'd hold a meeting in the Netflix theater, with everybody sitting on benches in a forum style. He would ask a few people in advance to be prepared to argue different sides of an issue. Eric Colson recalled to me, "These were really well-argued cases, and we'd be sitting there thinking, *Yeah, we should do that*, and then Reed would say, 'Okay, so-and-so, what's the counterargument?' And then we'd nod along with that person thinking, *Yeah, we should definitely do that!* You learn that the tough issues are never one-sided."

In that meeting the team would also break out into small groups of three or four to debate approaches to a problem and then present their solutions; any domain specialists in the topic to be debated would be spread around so as not to unduly sway opinion or cause others to hold back. Breaking out into smaller groups had multiple benefits. It cut down on the group-think that tends to prevail in larger groups, and it forced everyone to speak up, because in such a small group, hanging back and staying silent is glaringly conspicuous. It also allowed people from different working groups to get to know one another's personalities and ways of thinking. Additionally, it helped counteract the danger of expertise. As Eric said to me, "The downside of experts is that they are all too aware of the current constraints. Someone with fresh eyes can sometimes find their way around constraints, almost out of ignorance."

You can orchestrate great conversations if you take a little time to set them up right and make it clear that everyone is seeking the best answer for the customer and the company, that no one is arguing simply to win. The way to do that is to set the context: to be clear about what the group is going to decide and the reason for the conversation. If the discussion digresses, or if someone is stubbornly digging in, you can always interject, "What problem are we trying to solve here?" or "What leads you to believe that's true?"

One of best ways of ensuring that debates adhere to these standards, and stay civil, is to stage them in front of a group. So often executives keep their disagreements among themselves, yet those differences of opinion might be the most important things for those below the executive level to understand and weigh in on. Staging formal debates also models how good debating is done. Of course, this can be hard for people. They're often going to lose the day, and that's hard for anyone to do in front of a crowd, let alone really smart people who are extremely talented at problem solving and marshaling facts. But over time everyone comes to appreciate that they always come out alive and usually the best decision gets made.

Also, what better opportunity for employees to learn and grow than to watch, and participate in, such wrangling with the most pressing issues the company faces—and with the company's best minds and most qualified experts? This is a way to show people what excellence is, what a good argument looks like, and what presenting a strong case requires. It's also a great way to discover who your most talented people are. In the Culture Deck we wrote that one of the core qualities we looked for in those we hired and promoted was good judgment, defined, in essence, as the ability to make good decisions in ambiguous conditions, to dig deeply into the causes of problems, and to think strategically and articulate that thinking. Nothing could hone those skills better than this kind of open, vigorous debate. It also develops another of the core competencies we looked for: courage. People are emboldened to speak up when they see that their views will be heard and they can really make a difference.

Steve McLendon made another great point about the payoffs of open debate: younger workers (those pesky millennials), whom so many managers find so challenging, take to this transparency and encouragement to ask questions like moths to a flame. Steve has moved on from Netflix and is now a cofounder of 60dB, a start-up that streams personalized audio content, along with fellow former Netflixer John Ciancutti and onetime host of NPR's *Planet Money* Steve Henn. After leaving Netflix for other companies, Steve McLendon and John Ciancutti both encountered upper-management resistance to instituting the Netflix approach to questioning and open debate. So have other Netflixers who've moved on. (I was actually called to consult to the CEO of a company that two former Netflixers had joined; he couldn't contain his irritation with their questioning, shouting at me, "These god****ed Netflix people want to know everything! It's none of their god****ed business!") Steve was told it's not good to argue in front of employees because "it's like seeing your parents fight." But as he said, "The Netflix culture lends itself to managing younger people much more than the old top-to-bottom style." He's been hiring lots of very junior people, as start-ups generally do, and he's found that they are eager to learn about the whole business and that the transparency really resonates with them. They are the wave of the future, and it's in every business leader's interest to figure out how to capitalize on that thirst for knowledge.

I cautioned earlier about the limited value of formal employee-development practices such as conflict-resolution and management classes. There is simply no comparison between the learning employees may take away from such courses and what they'll gain from participating in debates about business decisions. Ask anyone at your company whether they'd rather spend a day in a negotiation seminar or be able to ask—with impunity—a tough but fair question of a high-level manager at a big company meeting or engage in a serious debate with their managers about the problem they're being asked to solve. I promise you, nobody but nobody is going to choose the seminar.

IN BRIEF

▶ Intense, open debate over business decisions is thrilling for teams, and they will respond to the opportunity to engage in it by offering the very best of their analytical powers.

▶ Set terms of debate explicitly. People should formulate strong views and be prepared to back them up, and their arguments should be based primarily on facts, not conjecture.

▶ Instruct people to ask one another for explanations of their views and of the problems being debated, rather than making assumptions about these things.

▶ Be selfless in debating. That means being genuinely prepared to lose your case and openly admitting when you have.

▶ Actually orchestrate debates. You can have people formally present cases, maybe even have them get up onstage. Try having people argue the opposing side, poking holes in their own position. Formal debates, for which people prepare, often lead to breakthrough realizations.

▶ Beware of data masquerading as fact; data is only as good as the conclusions it allows you to draw from it. People will be drawn to data that supports their biases. Hold your data up to rigorous scientific standards.

▶ Debates among smaller groups are often best because everyone feels freer to contribute—and it's more noticeable if they don't. Smaller groups also aren't as prone to groupthink as large groups are.

QUESTIONS TO CONSIDER

- What problem is your team working on, or what decision do you have coming up, that you could stage a formal debate over?

- Having set the rule that people must state their case by marshaling facts, will you be prepared to concede that someone on your team makes a stronger case than yours?

- Are there members of your team who have become too fixed in their views about an issue and whom you could ask to take the perspective of the other side in a debate in front of your team?

- How well is your team set up to conduct formal testing of ideas and to obtain the data they need to draw strong conclusions? Are there any ways in which you could provide them with access to tools they may lack?

- How can you help your people to consider data beyond the information that is familiar to them and that they know how to interpret? What biases might members of your team—and you— have about which data you should be considering and your interpretations of it?

- Can you invite younger members of your team, and perhaps of other teams, to listen in on some of your debates? Could you or their direct manager coach them about how to participate themselves?

- Can you establish a regular forum for the presentation of arguments about key decisions and the best ways to solve problems your team is working on?

CHAPTER FIVE

Build the Company *Now* That You Want to Be *Then*

| *Relentlessly Focus on the Future* |

Discussing the military's performance during the Iraq war, Donald Rumsfeld, the defense secretary at the time, famously said, "You go to war with the army you have, not the army you might want or wish to have at a later time." When I talk to managers about creating great teams, I tell them to approach the process in exactly the opposite way. You've got to hire *now* the team you wish to have in the future.

Many leaders are great at seeing the future of product development and competition. They work hard to assess what market demand will be and focus intensely on getting the product right and to market at the right time. But I find that they rarely look to the future in thinking about the team they'll need. They tend to focus on what their current team is achieving and how much more that team can do. If they do consider the future team, they generally think too much in terms of sheer numbers: *We need ten more engineers* or *We've got to double our sales team.*

I recently got a call from a CEO whose company now employs 150 people. He told me that it's going to grow to 300 and asked for my advice on getting to that number. It's a terrific company with a great product, and he told me they've got good funding. I'm sure they're going to grow fast, but how they're going to grow is the question. I said, "That's a precise number; what's it based on?" He said they were going to do twice as much work. I asked if the new people would need to do the same kinds of work as the current staff or if there might be new things to be done. Were they going to be launching a new product line, perhaps? If the teams were getting bigger, might he need more experienced managers? Did he want to keep teams smaller and maintain a flatter management structure? Did twice as much work mean they'd be reaching twice as many customers? If so, they'd have to significantly ramp up their customer service operation. But that might not mean hiring twice as many representatives; maybe outsourcing to a specialty firm would be better. Then I asked the question that I've found is the most thought-provoking for people in these consultations. He had said he needed 150 new people, so I asked, "Are you sure you don't want seventy-five people who you pay twice as much because they have twice as much experience and can be higher performers?"

Don't Let Hiring Become a Numbers Game

If you're not constantly engaging in this exercise of looking ahead and envisioning the team you'll need, your team leaders are inevitably going to end up in a zero-sum competition for people. Here's how it typically went in my experience.

A department head would call me and request approval to hire more people, and I'd say, "Well, make a business case and we'll discuss it." Ten minutes later he'd be at my door saying, "I don't think you understand. I need to talk to finance right now because we need fifteen more people in my organization or we're just not going to make it. We need them, we're going to demand them, and we're going to get them right now!" "Okay," I'd say, "great, fifteen more people at $150K a person. That's a million dollars, which isn't in your budget. Just to be clear, we have no money tree, so we can't just harvest a million bucks. We're going to have to get it from some other team. Are you asking for ten people when you really only need three?" I can't tell you how many times I would go back to people's projections and find that they had requested the budget for 10 or 15 percent more hires than they ended up making.

On the flip side, there's the problem of needing to hire people in too much of rush because you're caught short. I'd have to say to hiring managers all the time, "Let's look at everybody you hired last year. You brought in twenty people in one quarter, and five of them were wrong for the job because you were in such a rush." Other times they were very picky but hadn't been creating a pipeline of potential hires, so we couldn't find good enough people in time and actually had to postpone a project. Building the muscle to hire great people is a huge competitive advantage.

Don't Expect That Your Current Team Can Be Your Team for Tomorrow

Another mistake I've seen in building teams is assuming that current employees will be able to grow into the responsibilities of the future. This is an especially acute problem for start-ups, because founders often feel a strong sense of loyalty to their early team. When I'm consulting to start-up founders, I often have to tell them that many of their people aren't going to be competent in the new world order they're heading into as they scale. Usually they respond, "But I like them and they work hard and they're really great!" But the questions are: Can they do the job at scale? Are you going to need them to do tomorrow the same job they're doing now? What's your plan for them?

Though the problem is more acute for start-ups, it happens in all kinds of companies, no matter how mature. With the fast pace of innovation in business today, no one can afford to make this mistake.

I learned this lesson the hard way at Netflix. When we realized suddenly that within a year we would need the capacity to handle traffic equivalent to a third of U.S. Internet bandwidth at that time, we had to immediately begin formulating a new plan to increase our data capacity.

Right after that meeting, our head of product told me we needed to talk to IT immediately about getting set up with a cloud service. The IT guys essentially told us, "Why don't you go exec something and we'll build your cloud? We can do this." And I said, "To be honest, if anyone could do it, it's you guys, but you can't do it in nine months."

Recognizing what the time constraint meant in terms of the team we needed was crucial. This became a really important debate in the company, and we quickly realized that we were going to need a data team significantly different from the one we had. But the beautiful thing was that I could say, "It's okay, we've got six to nine months to figure it out." And we did. We brought in people with fantastic experience in cloud operations and made a deal with Amazon Cloud Services rather than trying to build our own system.

In my experience, one of the most important questions business leaders must regularly ask is "Are we limited by the team we have not being the team we *should* have?"

Fast-forward Six Months

Over time I developed the following method for addressing this challenge, which I share with every company I consult with. Imagine six months from now, you have the most amazing team you ever assembled and you're saying to yourself, *Wow, those guys are awesome! I can't believe what they're accomplishing.* (I say six months from now because that's about as far ahead as anyone can imagine in any business these days.)

First write down what the team will be accomplishing six months from now that it's not accomplishing now. Use all the figures you want. You can say you're making $X more revenue, the software is less buggy, you're closing the books in four days, whatever it is. Make a movie of it in your head. You're walking around the company watching this amazing team accomplishing these amazing things. Maybe they're working on a prototype of a big new product. Maybe you're walking around your shiny new warehouse and people are zipping around shipping twice as much product with the latest smart technology. Now, more important, think about how things are being done differently from the way they are currently done. Are people having more meetings or fewer?

Are they having big, loud debates? Are they making decisions faster? Who is making the decisions? Who's not? Are more people working quietly, heads down, in their own little spaces, or are they scribbling away like mad on whiteboards in groups all around? Are they working more cross-functionally? Doing more collaborative problem solving? When I do this exercise with clients, I ask them to actually close their eyes, and it's like I can see them walking through their company.

Then I say, "Okay, in order for those different things to be happening, what would people need to know how to do?" It might be something as simple as speaking up and having an argument and winning it. Or maybe being better at shutting up and listening. Or perhaps being more disciplined about communication. Maybe you need people who can launch a new product line of connected devices, or who know how to negotiate a certain kind of deal. What kind of skills and experience would it take for the team to operate the way you're envisioning and accomplish the things you'll need to do in that future?

This exercise often exposes problems in readiness regarding multiple changes to come, often changes that are rapidly closing in. Your team might lack the right hard skills. Or you might lack people with the soft skills or the right experience to be great managers. An essential question is, do you have enough capacity builders? By which I mean people who know how to build a great team. Bringing in great capacity builders was one of my main missions at Netflix. If you do that, they will tell you what teams you need and build them for you when you need them.

I think most business managers at most levels can pretty readily imagine the operational and managerial changes involved in doubling in size, maybe even tripling. Those with an exceptional aptitude for understanding complexity can imagine even larger-scale development of their businesses. But what if the size of your operations is going to increase tenfold in the next year, and you have a team of people who have seen only incremental growth? They probably won't know how to get there in time. You'll need people who can manage growth at the rate you're anticipating. Or what if you're evolving to a new business model?

After asking yourself these questions—and only after— look at the team you have. This will help you see the skills and experience of your team more accurately. You'll be more cognizant of what they don't know how to do, or don't do well, and you'll see where you need to bring in top performers in areas where you don't have them or don't have enough of them.

The basic problem is that most people start with the team they have, thinking, *We'll do more, and we'll be amazing.* The thing is, if you start with the team you have, sure you can do more, but it won't necessarily be amazing. Instead, build the ideal team by starting with the vision down the road. Identify the problem you want to solve, the time frame in which you want to solve it, the kinds of people who will be successful at that, and what they need to know how to do, then ask yourself, *What do we need to do to be ready and able, and whom do we need to bring in?*

You're Building a Team, Not Raising a Family

As Reed and I worked on clarifying what kind of culture we had to build to enable the speed of change we needed, we realized it was important that everyone understand we were going to make sure our teams were constantly evolving. In discussing this, we decided to use the metaphor that the company was like a sports team, not a family. Just as great sports teams are constantly scouting for new players and culling others from their lineups, our team leaders would need to continually look for talent and reconfigure team makeup. We set the mandate that their decisions about whom to bring in and who might have to go must be made purely on the basis of the performance their teams needed to produce in order for the company to succeed. If training people and grooming them to step into new roles was the best option, we fully backed that and we helped managers learn those skills. We also wanted them to carefully consider whether the best option might be bringing in new people who were high performers with the skills needed, even if that meant current team members would have to move on from the company.

Training well and spotting growth potential are vital skills for team leaders. I was always looking for hidden talents in people that would allow us to give them the opportunity to grow, and I encouraged all of our team leaders to do the same. Sometimes these gifts were obvious, but often they weren't, even to the employees themselves.

Rochelle King was someone who I could see had an important talent that we really needed and that she herself didn't fully recognize. Her expertise was as a designer and manager of designers, and we brought her in to manage that team when it really needed help. She whipped it into great shape incredibly fast, and I saw that she had the ability to take a dysfunctional team and make it highly well functioning. So within nine months of her joining, we asked her to lead two additional teams, one for enhanced metadata, the other for content operations. These were big teams, and she had no expertise in those areas. She said to me, "You understand that I've never run teams like these before?" But I was confident that she would step up and do a great job, and she did. Still, we were also both aware that her taking the job on was a risk, and we were honest about that.

When I spoke with Eric Colson, he recalled Reed offering him a big new job—managing the general data team—which Eric turned down three times before he finally accepted it. He had been writing algorithms to improve our operations systems and had been killing it. This job was a whole different ball game; he'd be managing a large company-wide team and reporting directly to Reed. He didn't think he was ready for it, but Reed was pretty convinced Eric could be great in the role. Eric thrived.

Promoting people gives them opportunities to stretch and take on new roles. It can be ideal, but it is not always the best option. We told our team leaders that it was important to be realistic about what sort of performance improvement people were capable of, and whether that could be achieved in the time needed.

We had a rule of thumb for whether to promote from within or bring in a top performer from outside: did the job to be done require expertise that no one inside had, or was the work in an area that we were ourselves at the forefront of innovating? With cloud services, there was better expertise outside, so it was much more effective for us to bring people in. With developing data algorithms, we were at the forefront of innovation and saw that in Eric we had a top-rate talent inside. With other roles, if we hadn't brought talent in from outside, we would almost surely have stumbled.

Sometimes Promoting Is Not the Right Solution

When I consult to company leaders and their team managers, probably the most difficult advice for them to accept is that they don't owe their people anything more than ensuring that the company is making a great product that serves the customer well and on time. They don't owe people the chance to take on a role they're not prepared for and don't have the talents for. They don't owe them a different job created to reward them for their service. And they certainly don't owe them holding the company back from making the personnel changes needed to thrive. I know this may sound harsh, because the notion that companies should make special investments in developing people, provide paths for promotion, and strive for high employee retention rates are deeply ingrained. But I've come to believe such thinking is outmoded and isn't even the best approach for employees. It often leads to people becoming stuck in jobs they don't really want or aren't doing as well as they want to—or as you need them to—rather than scouring the job landscape for better opportunities.

Giving people promotions and coaching them in new roles can be both enormously satisfying for team leaders and great for performance. But promoting and developing people are also often simply not the best things for team performance. Managers should not be expected to be career planners. In today's fast-moving business environment, trying to play that role can be dangerous.

At Netflix, when we were interviewing people, we told them straight out that we were not a career-management company, that we believed people's careers were theirs to manage, and that while there might be lots of opportunity for them to advance at the company, we wouldn't be designing opportunities for them. So often companies give people half of a job they need done, because the person can't do the whole job. I realized that we just couldn't afford to do that. We needed people who could do the whole job. We were also determined not to make the incredibly common mistake of promoting into management roles strong performers who are simply not well suited to managing.

In some periods of a company's growth there is lots of opportunity for current employees to be promoted into new roles. But often there are simply no legitimate spots for people, even very good people, to move up into. When there were openings at Netflix that we might have promoted people into, in many instances we knew the much better option was to bring in someone who had already been a top performer in the job we needed done. If people were eager to take on responsibilities we couldn't give them, or to do work that wasn't a priority for us, we encouraged them to look for those opportunities elsewhere. We also suggested that our employees interview elsewhere regularly, so that they could gauge the market of opportunities. This also allowed us to get a better understanding of how sought after they were and what we should be paying them. The advantages of more fluid team building flow both ways.

I believe the best advice for all working people today is to stay limber, to keep learning new skills and considering new opportunities, regularly taking on new challenges so that work stays fresh and stretches them. At Netflix we encouraged people to take charge of their own growth, availing themselves of the rich opportunities we afforded them to learn from stellar colleagues and managers and making their own way, whether that meant rising within the company or seizing a great opportunity elsewhere.

Put Yourself in a Start-up Founder's Shoes

I appreciate that embracing this perspective can be a struggle, and for good reason. We've been taught to think so differently about our responsibilities to our employees. I see this most intensely with the start-up founders I advise. They almost always have to face the hard truth that the kinds of people and the ways of working they needed in the early phase of developing the product and finding a market are very different from the people and the talents that will allow their company to scale. In the beginning, they need the smartest people they can afford to pay, who want to work very hard and who believe in their vision. The belief part is crucial, because all start-ups are crazy ideas. If they were logical, somebody else would be doing them. Initial start-up success requires making all kinds of mistakes and being willing to keep working incredibly hard trying all sorts of things, really pounding at it, until you have a product that's viable and a market that's receptive. The answers are unknown and most of the work is improvisational. Then, suddenly, growth starts to take off and the problems are not so much ones solved by trial and error as ones requiring experience. They are problems of scale and complexity. And the thing about scale and complexity is that sometimes you get lucky and some of those early people can cope with the changes and develop the skills needed, but many can't or don't want to.

Virtually every company is contending with this same challenge all the time to some degree—the challenge of recognizing that change has to happen and new people will be needed to bring it about. If this perspective is uncomfortable for you, ask yourself, *What would be the right thing for a start-up founder to do in the face of this challenge?* Why should that answer be any different for you?

Nostalgia Is an Early Warning Sign

One reason Reed and I started using the "team not family" metaphor was that as the company kept changing, we saw that nostalgia for the good old scrappy days was a powerful force of resistance.

The nostalgia was totally understandable; I had it too. The early days of Netflix were a blast. We were so informal that we had company meetings around a picnic table in the parking lot. And we were a brash upstart in a cool business. We loved going to the Sundance Film Festival and presenting edgy movies by up-and-coming directors. I remember fondly the glee with which Ted Sarandos told me one year that he'd snagged the director's cut of a much-buzzed-about and quite graphic black comedy for screening, titled *Spun*. The movie was set in the meth culture of Eugene, Oregon, and depicted the perils of addiction with brutal honesty. Being the edgy appreciators of such boundary-pushing films was in the company's DNA and was a source of pride for many of us. When we made the move to streaming, all of a sudden we were going to reinvent television. *So much for the ultrahip indie film company,* many thought, and some people weren't at all happy about it. Of course, as Netflix has moved into original content creation, it's become strikingly clear that going into television didn't expunge that edgy soul at all. Shows like *Orange Is the New Black* and *The Santa Clarita Diet,* about a suburban wife who is a human-flesh-eating zombie, have demonstrated the company still loves pushing the envelope.

An appreciation of the core elements of a company's early success is so important, and it can be retained as companies adapt and grow. But nostalgia that inspires resistance to change will fuel discontent and often undermine growth. In the early days of Netflix, an engineer who'd been there from early on said to me, "You know, it's not like it used to be when we all used to hang in the parking lot and everyone contributed to the product; now people don't know each other's names. It's getting really big, and I just don't think management understands that things have changed." I was management, of course, so I assured him that we were very much aware. Because he had shared that thought with me several times and I could see how upsetting the changes were for him, I then asked him, "Do you know why things are changing?" And he responded, "Why?" I said, "Because we're successful! Do you know what we want to be someday? We want to be a global corporation!" That's a shocking term to a hard-core start-up guy. Sometimes people who were just right for an organization at a certain point and loved working for it are best off moving to a new organization with a similar set of challenges and environment. I told this engineer, "It's okay. You don't have to be part of it. You may be most happy in a fifty-person organization. Maybe that's where you find your greatest joy."

Taking this approach to team building meant that at Netflix I had to develop a new approach to hiring so we would have the strong talent pipeline we needed. We had to build organization-wide capacity for excellent hiring, and we did.

IN BRIEF

▶ To stay agile and move at the speed of change, hire the people you need for the future *now*.

▶ On a regular basis, take the time to envision what your business must look like six months from now in order to be high-performing. Make a movie of it in your head, imagining how people are working and the tools and skills they have. Then start immediately making the changes necessary to create that future.

▶ More people will not necessarily do more work or better work; it's often better to have fewer people with more skills who are all high performers.

▶ Successful sports teams are the best model for managers; they are constantly scouting for new talent and culling their current roster. You're building a team, not raising a family.

▶ Some members of your team may simply not be able to grow into high performers for the future you're heading to. It is not the job of the business to invest in developing them; the job is to develop the product and market.

▶ Develop and promote from within when that's the best option for performance; when it's better to hire from outside, be proactive in doing so.

▶ The ideal is for people to take charge of developing themselves; this drives optimal growth for both individuals and companies.

QUESTIONS TO CONSIDER

- Have you systematically assessed the skills of all members of your team against the capabilities you will need in six months to a year?

- Are there some ways of working—such as programming and working with robots, collaborating cross-functionally, or mapping out and redesigning the customer experience—in which you can foresee your team will need strong experience?

- Would your team's performance be significantly boosted if you brought in a new top performer, or several, even if the cost of those hires would mean scaling down the size of your team?

- What opportunities do you see on the horizon that your team could begin capitalizing on now if you brought in some new talent? Perhaps there is a new technology that would allow you to offer a new or better service or product. Maybe a competitor is leaving market share vulnerable or a new market is developing.

- In which areas is your team or company at the vanguard of innovation, with leading talent spearheading the effort, and in which are you running as fast as you can to catch up, or soon will find yourself in that situation if you don't make some new hires?

- How much of your time are you spending on the development of your team's skills, and how satisfied are you with how quickly people are getting up to the speed you need?

CHAPTER SIX

Someone Really Smart in Every Job

| *Have the Right Person in Every Single Position* |

At Netflix we had three fundamental tenets to our talent-management philosophy. First, the responsibility for hiring great people, and for determining whether someone should move on, rested primarily with managers. Second, for every job, we tried to hire a person who would be a great fit, not just adequate. Finally, we would be willing to say good-bye to even very good people if their skills no longer matched the work we needed done.

As John Ciancutti, who was one of our best hiring managers, said to me, "Knowing when it's time for people to move on goes hand in hand with bringing in top performers with the skills you need. They are two sides of the same coin. If you are not great at hiring high-talent people, then you cannot truly be comfortable letting good people go. You will never be good at one without the other and will never be good at building a high-performance team." This approach allowed us to dynamically and proactively create the teams we needed to reach the goals we were heading toward, not getting bogged down by teams that were outmoded and struggling desperately to evolve.

John totally embraced our talent-management philosophy, and he has taken it with him in his endeavors since leaving Netflix, such as building up a team at Coursera and staffing the team at 60dB, which he currently runs. He wrote a great piece for *First Round Review* about his specific tactics for hiring great people, "This Is How Coursera Competes Against Google and Facebook for the Best Talent," which I highly recommend. His passion for the subject and his development of such detailed methods speaks to how seriously so many of our hiring managers took their team-building responsibility. In fact, we stressed to all hiring managers that building a great team was their *most* important job. My HR team and I closely coached them about how to do great sourcing and interviewing; how to close the deal with candidates; how to evaluate when to part ways; and how to talk about the decision not only to that person but also to the rest of the team.

Be a Great Company to Be From

That early morning Reed called to ask me to join Netflix, after I asked him to tell me what his ideal company would be, he asked me the same question. I told him that my ideal company would be one that was a great place to be from, like having been at Apple or Microsoft in the early days. I said that because I have seen two consistent truths about the best companies and the best employees. The most competitive companies are able to stay limber, always innovating and growing, largely because they are always proactively bringing in the new talent they need. The best employees are always looking for challenging new opportunities, and though they are usually intensely loyal, many of them will eventually seek those opportunities elsewhere. You can never know when they might decide to make a move, and often there is nothing you'll be able to do to stop them.

Earlier I mentioned Eric Colson. In less than three years, he rose from a data analyst position to the role of VP of data science and engineering, reporting directly to Reed and managing four big and very important teams. He had never expected to be given so much responsibility, certainly not so fast. He told me recently that he was, and still is, hugely grateful for the opportunities offered to him. He also loved the work he was doing at Netflix. He was managing teams at the forefront of applying all the sexy new tools of "big data," like machine learning. Yet he came to me one day after three years in that role and told me he was going to work for a tiny start-up called Stitch Fix, which uses data analysis combined with input from personal stylists to send clients recommended clothes for purchase. I thought, *What??? He's going to work on shipping clothing in boxes?* "Eric, are you all right?" He said the company was going to be like the Netflix of clothes. I still didn't get it and asked him why he was interested. All of a sudden he lit up with the possibilities, and I said to him, "You're in love with the data, aren't you?" He left, and as Stitch Fix's chief algorithms officer he has led the development of highly innovative algorithms and a novel approach to combining machine learning with human stylists' insights that have propelled the company to rapid growth.

We tried very, very hard to keep great people at Netflix whose skills and experience we needed, but we were operating in an extremely competitive talent pool. We recognized that we had to be highly proactive about creating a pipeline of top talent. On the flip side, because of how fast our business was changing, we also had to be willing to part with people whose skills were no longer needed, even if they had done a great job and were wonderfully talented. Our overriding talent-management mandate had to be building the best team for the future we were creating.

This is why I say that retention is not a good metric by which to evaluate your team-building success or whether you've created a great culture. The measure should be not simply how many people you are keeping but how many great people you have with the skills and experience you need. How many of *them* you are keeping? How many new people with the skills and experience you need are you hiring? You also want to closely monitor how rigorously you are evaluating whom you need to replace and how efficiently you're acting on that determination.

I'm not saying that adopting this perspective and reliably acting on it is easy. It's hard enough letting people go who aren't performing. It's even more difficult to let go people who have done a great job. But what helps is knowing that they have a great résumé because they've worked for you. That will be a huge assist in finding a great next job. You can also actively help them. The single best way in which companies can ensure that people who leave are able to find great opportunities elsewhere is to make the company one that is known to be intensely driven to hire top talent. If managers operate this way, they can become masterful at good good-byes. More on that in chapter eight. For now, let's focus on great hellos.

Great Work Is Not About the Perks

The Perk Wars have escalated to an absurd level. A few months ago, I was asked to come speak to the whole staff of a start-up, probably a hundred people. During the Q&A after my talk, one of the employees raised his hand and said, "I have a very important question to ask you: how do you feel about departmental kegerators versus a company kegerator?" At the time, this company had swings and hammocks strewn around its offices. To this audience member I responded, "What kind of question is that? You know how business works, right?" He said, "I don't understand what you're asking." And I told him, "Well, you make a service available to your customers and they give you money for it. That money pays for the costs of operating, and what's left over is profit. That is the essence of business. It has nothing to do with kegerators. Companies don't exist to make happy employees!" I looked around the room and people were clearly shocked. I then explained that it's absolutely great for employees to be happy, but that it's best for both them and their companies if the reason they're happy is that they're doing great work with great people.

I've actually been asked by one executive, "Should I worry that we don't have a bartender or a personal chef?" If someone wants to walk out your door and go to another company because it serves better craft beer, you should just say to that person, "Have fun! Oh, and let's do happy hour at your place soon."

People's happiness in their work is not about gourmet salads or sleeping pods or foosball tables. True and abiding happiness in work comes from being deeply engaged in solving a problem with talented people you know are also deeply engaged in solving it, and from knowing that the customer loves the product or service you all have worked so hard to make.

Money Doesn't Buy Love

We decided over time at Netflix to pay highly competitive salaries. We had to compete with Google and Facebook and

Amazon for top technical talent, and we believed in paying top dollar for the talented people we needed. But we did *not* want to be competing on price as a core lever of convincing people to join the company. Word certainly got around that we paid very well, and there is no question that this helped us to bring in the people we wanted, but we had a rule that we would not discuss compensation with candidates until we knew they wanted to accept an offer. We would talk about our philosophy on compensation, but we would not talk numbers.

In my experience, when people bring up money fairly early in the interviewing process, they either are underpaid in their current job, are being paid very well and are worried that you won't be able to improve on that, or are primarily interested in the money and not truly passionate about the job. We had no interest in hiring people because they were being underpaid and we could get their talents on the cheap. We were also generally not concerned that we would be unable to make a high enough offer if we really wanted to hire the person. We had not set up a rigid compensation system as so many companies do, with their bell curve distributions and 6 percent merit increase budgets and strict salary bands. We were free to offer what we needed to offer. So we had no good reason to talk numbers up front. As for candidates who were mostly interested in the money, we wanted to weed them out. We would tell them, "We don't think you're right for us. We think at this point in your career it's important for you to chase the money. If that's what's up, then go to one of our competitors!"

We also did not have a bonus system. If your employees are adults who put the company first, an annual bonus won't make them work harder or smarter. We handled equity compensation in a completely different way than most companies do. We allowed employees to tell us what portion of their compensation they wanted in stock options, and rather than adding those onto their salary, the amount was in lieu of a portion their salary. In addition, rather than using stock options as "golden handcuffs," we imposed no vesting period. Options would vest on a monthly basis. Those options were available to exercise for ten years, allowing for long-term increase in the stock price.

I was talking to Warby Parker CEO Neil Blumenthal, and he told me that he wanted my advice about creating an executive bonus program. I asked him, "Okay, you want it to be a combination of equity and cash?" Yep. "And you want it to be based on company goals, team goals, department goals, and individual goals." Yep. Then I asked him, "Didn't you tell me when we talked last that you're opening up more stores, and didn't we discuss how there was a fifty-fifty chance that the strategy was going to work out? So now you want to set up a very complicated system that you have to explain to finance and you have to explain to the board and you have to explain to the stock committee. If they agree, then you have to set up software so you can track results versus goals, when you know that you don't really know whether those goals are realistic." He said, "But I want to reward them." And I said, "Well, if you hit all your targets and everything works out, great; give them a ton of money. Throw stock at them. You don't need a bonus system tied to goals. I know you and I know your team and I know that a bonus program is not going to incent them to do anything they're not going to do anyway."

Motivation Is About Talent Density and Appealing Challenges

We didn't understand right away at Netflix that great colleagues and tough challenges to tackle were the strongest draws to working at the company. But very early on we understood that we had to be really rigorous about maintaining our talent density. We couldn't make any promises to people about long-term careers at the company. We were quite open about that, and over time we found that it was no deterrent to attracting top performers. When I talked to John Ciancutti about this, he beautifully expressed what we hoped would be the way employees thought about our approach: "After the 2001 layoff, the talent density at the company became amazing. The executive team started to talk about how Netflix was a company where there are amazing people who are high functioning and can go on and do great things at other places. What I heard was 'Don't expect there to be a long-term path for you.' But working with amazing people and the opportunity to grow were more important to me than having an explicit promise of a path for promotion."

The Diversity of Brilliance

Netflix was always being compared to Google, and we often competed for the same talent, but the two companies have totally different approaches to hiring, because they have such different approaches to growing their businesses. Google was a tough, tough competitor to go up against for hiring managers, but we were able again and again to bring in top talent that might have gone to Google because we articulated so clearly what our approach to building teams and managing people was and didn't try to compete on Google's terms.

I worked with Eric Schmidt at Sun, and I realized that Google reminded me of the go-go days at Sun, when we focused primarily on hiring as many amazing people as we could, but that Google was even better at doing that because it had such a broad goal: to organize all the world's info. I mean, can you have a broader goal than that? So it makes great sense for Google to hire as many smart people as it can, put them in an environment where they have all the resources they could need, ask them to bubble up tons of ideas, and skim the best of those off the top. Its leaders want to drive the company forward in many different ways; quantity for them matters a great deal. At Netflix we were doing essentially one thing, so we needed exactly the right people with the right skills and experience to do their part of that one thing. I would say to people in the recruiting process, "If you want your mind to be free and want to think of all kinds of radical things that may or may not happen, then Google is the place for you. We do one thing. We exist to serve our customers' happiness as a result of that particular product. So if that's not your passion, then go to Google. It's a great company. It's just very different."

I really dislike the term "A player." It implies that there is some grading system that can determine who will be best for a position. HR people always ask me how Netflix manages to hire only A players. I say, "You know, there's this island that's populated exclusively by A players, and only some of us know where it is."

Making great hires is about making great matches. One company's A player may be a B player for another firm, and vice versa. There is no generic formula for what makes people successful, despite a great deal of effort and all sorts of assessments to try to come up with one. Many of the people we let go from Netflix because they were not excelling at what we were doing at the time went on to excel at other jobs.

Finding the right people is also not primarily about "culture fit." What most people really mean when they think someone is a good culture fit is that the candidate is someone they'd like to have a beer with. That approach is often totally wrongheaded. People can have all sorts of different personalities and be great fits for the job you need done. One of our great hires was Anthony Park, who was working as a programmer for a bank in Arizona when we reached out to him. On paper he certainly didn't look like a slam-dunk fit. He was a "programmer," not a "software developer." He was also a pretty buttoned-up, quiet guy, so I worried a little about how he'd cope with our debate-like-crazy culture. We called him because someone told me he had created a Netflix-enhancing app, which he had posted on his website. We brought him in for a day of interviews, and everyone loved him as well as the app he'd created. When he got to me, shortly after we started talking he turned bright red. I asked him if he was okay, and he said, "You're going to make me an offer, aren't you?" And I said, "Yes, we are." He said, "And you're going to pay me a lot of money, right?" And I said, "Well, you're not programming for a bank anymore. You know, you'd be here in Silicon Valley and it's expensive to live out here. We're going to pay you commensurate with what it will take for you to have a great life with your family here." He seemed overwhelmed, and I asked again if he was all right. He said with amazement, "You're going to pay me a lot of money to do what I love to do!" I did wonder how he'd fit in with the high-powered team he was joining, and I hoped they wouldn't burn him out in a few weeks.

A few months later, I sat in on a meeting his team was having, and it was really intense. Everyone was arguing. He suddenly said, "Can I speak now?" The room went silent, because Anthony didn't talk much, but when he did, it was to say something really smart. Over time, everybody learned to pause and wait for him, and he would always say something that would make us all think, *Dammit, why didn't I think of that?* Now he's a vice president. Organizations can adapt to many people's styles; culture fit can work both ways.

Getting Under the Résumé

We had to be very creative about where we looked for talent, because we so often had to find people with rarefied technical skills. When we were looking for big-data experts, no one really even knew what "big" meant. We couldn't just search résumés and do keyword matching. Our recruiters had to imagine across the universe of all the different kinds of companies that handle masses of data. Many of them at first were insurance or credit card companies. What's more, our recruiting team didn't have much of the knowledge to probe into people's technical skills. Our best recruiter of technical people was Bethany Brodsky. She knew virtually nothing about technology before coming to Netflix, but she was great at understanding our business and the root problems that had to be solved, and she understood that more important than the match of a person's prior experience was the match of their approach to problem solving.

Bethany told me that one of her best interviews was with a guy we ended up hiring who was working at Lawrence Livermore Laboratory, a government research center that focuses on nuclear science. This was when Netflix was first getting into streaming and was on only a few devices: Xbox, Roku, and TiVo. In interviews, Bethany told candidates that we had signed up a million new subscribers in just thirty days on one of those three devices, and she asked which one they thought it was. TiVo was really taking off then, so most people said, "TiVo for sure." But this guy asked her whether there were any special conditions attached to getting a Netflix subscription on any of the devices. She told him that yes, in fact, for the Xbox you had to have a "gold membership." He then reasoned that it must be the Xbox: since those users were already willing to pay a premium, they would probably be more inclined to pay the extra for Netflix. He was right, and that's when she knew he was our guy.

I had a similar aha moment about a candidate when I interviewed Christian Kaiser, who worked at AOL managing a group of twenty-five programmers. I had talked to quite a few people from his group, because they were doing technical work similar to something we needed done. But they all wanted to stay at AOL. At this point Netflix was a much sexier place to work than AOL, so I was perplexed as to why they didn't want to move. When I asked them, they would say, "I have the most amazing boss! He's the best communicator I've ever known. I can't bear the thought of leaving him." So I said to my recruiters, "Go get that guy." I was amazed when he came in; not only did he have a very thick German accent, but he also stuttered. This guy was the great communicator? On top of that, he was clearly nervous; after all, he hadn't interviewed for many years. It was truly painful, for him and for me. But when I asked him if he could explain to me, in really simple terms, the incredibly complicated technical work he was doing, he just transformed. He still stuttered, but he gave me a riveting explanation, and I realized, *That's it! He's great at making really complicated things understandable.* He was an amazing team builder for Netflix. He also left teams he had built in order to lead new projects simply because they needed to get done. He redefined what "my team" meant by creating such good teams that they could carry on without him.

We always tried to be creative about probing more deeply with people, and also more deeply into their résumés. Bethany once decided to analyze the résumés of all the data science people we'd hired who were really good to see if she could find any common features, and she did: they shared an avid interest in music. From then on, she and her recruiting team would probe into people's interest in music when interviewing for those jobs.

She recalled, "We'd get really excited and call out, 'Hey, I found a guy who plays piano!'" She concluded that these people could easily toggle between their left brains and right brains, a great skill for data analysis.

Build a Culture of Hiring

The technical nature of our business at Netflix was a key reason it was important that managers be so engaged in the hiring process. But I think the same should be demanded at all companies. All hiring managers should understand, really deeply, what the company's approach to hiring is and how to execute on it, down to every detail. And this should be modeled from the top. Bethany once worked with Reed on filling a director position. They met on a Thursday morning to discuss what type of candidates they were looking for. The next afternoon, Reed sent her an email telling her he had sent messages to twenty prospects he had found on LinkedIn and had gotten three responses. He had also gone ahead and had a Skype session with one of them, really liked him, and wanted to have him come in on Monday.

When hiring managers are so engaged, that makes recruiters only all the more competitive. Bethany told me that after she got that message from Reed, she became determined to find someone even better. (We ended up hiring Reed's guy and Reed gloated about it for years.)

Our recruiters' job was to coach our hiring managers, and they created a slide deck to go over with every one of them, one on one. They would ask every hiring manager, "What's your interview process look like? What's your interview team look like? What's your structure around having people come in for interviews look like?" People don't have to approach interviewing or sourcing the same way. Our best hiring managers had all sorts of different ways of finding and fielding candidates. We had a saying, "Always be recruiting!" Candidates came from everywhere from professional conferences to the sidelines of a kids' soccer game to conversations on airplanes! But certain fundamentals should be strictly enforced. I set an ironclad rule that if anyone saw a stranger sitting by themselves waiting for an interview, they should stop and say, "Hi, I'm ____. Who are you? Are you here for an interview? Who are you waiting for? Let's take a look at your schedule for today and I'll help you find the next person." I knew the message was heard loud and clear because if I was ever late coming to meet with a candidate, and I said, "Sorry, I hope someone talked to you," they'd say, "Six people talked to me."

Interviews trumped any meeting that a hiring manager was scheduled for, and they were the only reason that attendees of our executive staff meeting could miss that meeting or leave it early. Really! Candidates are evaluating you just as you're evaluating them; people forget that.

Our goal was for every single person who came in for an interview to walk away wanting the job, even if we hated them. We wanted them to think, *Wow, that was an incredible experience. It was efficient, it was effective, it was on time, the questions were relevant, people were smart, and I was treated with dignity.* I would tell people, "Even if this person isn't the right fit, we might love their next-door neighbor."

In the end, it was the hiring manager's responsibility to make the decision. Team members would provide input. My team and I would also weigh in. But the ultimate responsibility was with that manager (as was the performance of the team they were building). We acted as quickly as possible once the decision was made. No running the hire by two levels of management, the compensation department, and HR for approval.

People from my team worked directly with hiring managers to determine compensation as well as title and any other details of offers. Recruiters laid the groundwork; managers made the offers. Speed and efficiency often meant we could close candidates who were interviewing with other great companies.

The interview and hiring process gives a powerful first impression about how your company operates, for good and for bad.

Your HR People Must Be Businesspeople

I was at a start-up the other day talking to their head of people, and she told me that they were planning an off-site to talk about how her team could be more effective in getting new employees up and running in their jobs. She asked me, "Should I invite the recruiters to the off-site?" She seriously didn't know whether or not the people whose specific job it was to assist in hiring new staff should be invited to the meeting about onboarding new staff. The sad truth is that most companies treat recruitment as a separate, nonbusiness, even non-HR function. And many young companies outsource it or have only people who are record keepers, ticket takers, administrators, and agenda fillers inside.

Over time our strategy evolved to creating an internal recruiting firm, and a top-quality one, because I wanted the highest-quality candidates possible. I brought in Jessica Neal from an outside firm to take charge of running that team. Building up a talented team was a substantial investment, but I was able to make an irrefutable business case for doing so. I could clearly show what the return would be from eliminating outside headhunter fees, and we saved bundles of money over time.

I also made it totally clear to the recruiting team that

they were considered vital contributors to building the business and they had to deeply understand the needs of the business. The flip side was that hiring managers really began to treat the HR team as their business partners.

I told my staff, "We are a service organization, but it's not spelled "S-E-R-V-A-N-T." We weren't in service to the hiring managers; we were in service to the customers of Netflix. I wanted my people to understand that they had to know the customers' needs and desires as well as the product managers' and marketers'. They also had to have the same level of understanding and feel a deep connection to creating the product.

One of the great cases of our recruiters playing a crucial role in building the business was when we wanted to get into the games business. We had to negotiate deals for every gaming device. We got the Xbox first and then wanted to get on the Nintendo Wii. This was another leap into a really different business for us. The development cycles for hardware devices were many years long, and we were an Internet company used to pushing new code every couple of weeks. When we finally got the good news that we had made a deal with Nintendo, I asked the head of the team developing for Wii, "So, have we got anybody here who knows anything about Nintendo hardware?" We didn't. When I asked him how much time we had to get our Wii products developed, he told me about eight months. If we didn't make that deadline, we would have to wait two years before we could get on the Wii.

I went to my office and immediately called Bethany and told her, "Stop what you're doing and come in here right now. We have to brainstorm how we're going to create a Wii team." Fast-forward eight months and we were having a big party celebrating our launch on the Wii. Bethany was standing next to me. I saw she was misty-eyed and asked her if anything was wrong. She said, "No, I built that team! I helped ship the Wii today!" When the team was asked to say a few words, they said, "Thanks to Bethany Brodsky, because without her we wouldn't be here today!" That was what I wanted our recruiters to feel about their contribution to the business and what I wanted all managers to feel about the value of our recruiters.

Getting them working optimally together requires holding hiring managers accountable. One day I overheard one of my best recruiters saying a new executive wasn't engaging with her in a serious way. "He doesn't return my calls. He doesn't return my emails. I send him résumés and he doesn't respond. I'm so frustrated, because we really need to build him a great team. I feel like I'm letting the company down." So I walked up to her and said, "I think you need to work with someone else. I'll take care of this." Then I sent him an email telling him that I had reassigned his recruiter: "I've put her on another project because you appear to have a methodology for hiring and don't seem to need her help. Let us know when we can step in and assist. Love, Patty." Within minutes he was at my desk fuming, "What the hell?" So I asked him, "Is it true that she set up two meetings with you and you canceled?" He snapped back, "I'm a busy guy, you know. I'm doing the work of ten people." So I asked, "Is it true that she sent you a number of qualified candidates and you didn't respond? Look, just so you know, it's your job to build to the team, not hers. By the way, there are three other people who are delighted that she's not spending time on you. She's amazing. She's a great partner. She can really make this work for you. But if you don't need her, that's cool."

It infuriates me when I hear hiring managers dismiss the value of good HR people. Usually when I would ask managers why they weren't engaging with recruiters more, they'd say, "Well, you know, they're not that smart and they don't really understand what's going on in my business or how the technology works." My response was "Well then start expecting—and demanding—that they do!" And hire people who *are* smart. If you hire smart people and you insist that they be businesspeople, and you include them in running the business, then they'll act like businesspeople.

I even occasionally advise companies to hire a businessperson to run HR, not an HR specialist. That person should be able to understand the details of your business and how you earn your revenue and who your customers are and your strategy for the future, just like any other department or division head. One of the reasons that I'm no fan of the annual performance review process is that not only does it take up a lot of your HR department's time, but it is so often removed from any true connection to business results and serving customers.

I asked one very senior HR executive from a Fortune 100 company that I consulted to, "Can you tell me what business metric is affected by the completion of your annual performance review?" He said, "I don't understand the question, Patty." I repeated, "What business metric is directly affected by the completion of the annual performance review?" He said, "Again, I'm not sure what you're asking." So I said, "Might it be revenue, growth, profit? You know, the metrics that we measure our businesses with." Then I asked him how much of his staff's time was consumed by the process, and he said, "I really have no idea! But it's worth it." Nowhere else in our companies are we allowed to justify something that takes such incredible effort with merely a feeling that "it's worth it."

Just imagine if instead of spending so much time on the review process, all of your people were spending that time collaborating to bring in extraordinary talent that accomplishes amazing products or services for your customers.

IN BRIEF

▶ Hiring great performers is a hiring manager's most important job. Hiring managers should actively develop their own pipelines of talent and take the lead in all aspects of the hiring process. They are the lead recruiters.

▶ The teams and companies most successful in staying ahead of the curve manage to do so because they proactively replenish their talent pool.

▶ Retention is not a good measure of team-building success; having a great person in every single position on the team is the best measure.

▶ Sometimes it's important to let even people who have done a great job go in order to make space for high performers in new functions or with different skills.

▶ Bonuses, stock options, high salaries, and even a clear path to promotion are not the strongest draw for high performers. The opportunity to work with teams of other high performers whom they'll learn from and find it exhilarating to work with is by far the most powerful lure.

- ► Making a great hire is not about bringing in an "A player"; it's about finding a great match for your needs. Someone who is a high performer for one team may not be for another team.

- ► Get beyond the résumé. Be really creative about where you look for talent. Dig further than a list of experiences. Consider wide-ranging experiences and focus on people's fundamental problem-solving abilities.

- ► Make the interviewing experience extremely impressive all the way through. You want every single person you interview to want to join the company at the end of the process.

- ► HR must be businesspeople who truly understand the way your business works, even if that's quite technical. They should be creative, proactive partners in the hiring process. Investing time in explaining to them the details of the talents you need will pay remarkable dividends.

QUESTIONS TO CONSIDER

- Can you name the two people you would call right away to talk to about taking the place of your top performers should they leave?

- What change is under way in your business? How prepared are you to begin interviewing for the new talent you need in the event the change happens faster than you've expected?

- How creative are you in looking for candidates? Have you devoted time to cultivating lead generators among your professional network? Do you consider finding candidates to be primarily your responsibility, or do you wait for recruiters to find them?

- How thoughtful and rigorous is the interview process your candidates go through?

- How well do you think the recruiters working with you understand the details of the jobs to be filled and the qualities you are looking for in hires?

CHAPTER SEVEN

Pay People What They're Worth *to You*

| Compensation Is a Judgment Call |

One of the most challenging topics that I consult about is compensation. Offering competitive salaries is obviously one of the requisites of hiring top talent. But while most every business would like to mark its salaries to the market, doing so is often a daunting challenge. We have plentiful resources to tap for salary information from a range of industry surveys, which cover every domain and offer an elaborate breakdown of levels. They're amazingly sophisticated. But the issue is that jobs are not widgets, and neither are people. Any role you need filled is likely specialized in ways that the survey job descriptions cannot possibly truly account for. Meanwhile, any potential recruit may have skills that can't be measured by surveys, like good judgment and collaborative prowess. Say you need a software engineer. Great, do you want a senior programmer fluent in the best new techniques in search engine development? And this person also has to know how to manage a staff of five? Oh, and you also need this person to understand online advertising systems well enough to work effectively with marketing on developing an online advertising strategy? A salary survey is not going to tell you how much such a person is paid—or should be paid *by you*.

Compensation departments end up spending gobs of time comparing descriptions and making the best calculations they can to adjust for all factors. But of course, that process still only gives you a baseline understanding of the true market landscape. How many people with that set of qualifications are available? Many times, as any HR professional or hiring manager knows all too well, to get the person you really want, you're going to have to essentially throw your calculations away and respond to actual market demand.

But I found that market demand is still not adequate as a guide to the compensation you should offer, because it is of the current moment, while hiring should be about the future. The way I like to think about this is that the prevailing compensation system is often in arrears; it's behind the curve in helping us calculate the value of many hires. Say that your recruiter manages to bring in the software engineer with all those particular credentials you need, and you all love her, but she has another offer from your main competitor and it's a good deal higher—let's say $35,000 more—than you've been prepared to pay. In determining what to offer, you should consider the difference it could make to the future of your business if you bring in this really great engineer with all of the skills and experience you need, rather than your second-choice candidate, who may be a quite distant second choice and whom it will take you another three months to hire because you'll keep looking for another person with all the skills and talents of your first choice.

How much extra revenue might that great first choice be able to help produce? Might she be able to ensure that you beat out your competitor on the launch of a fabulous new search system, especially if she gets started now instead of three months down the road? How much ad revenue might she help bring in by notching up your targeting? What about the value of her management experience? Might a really good member of her team who gets an offer at another firm decide to stay because she's a great team leader? That's not to mention the value to you of her *not* working for your competitor, especially if your domain is in a period of rapid innovation.

Neither current market demand nor salary surveys can help you calculate these future adds. I'm not saying that there is no value to benchmarking with salary surveys, but I do advise curtailing elaborate efforts to compare apples and oranges regarding what others are paying and to work out what others are paying now. It's better to focus more on what you can afford to pay for the performance you want and the future you're heading to.

Separate Performance Review and Compensation Systems

One of the first things I did at Netflix was to decouple our pay system from the feedback process. I appreciate that it's difficult to accept that this is possible, let alone advisable. The systems have become seemingly inextricably intertwined. Indeed, the tight bond between the performance review process and salary increase and bonus calculations is one of the main factors holding companies back from doing away with the review process. Which is one of the good reasons for decoupling the systems.

Resistance to the notion of disassociating them stems largely from what seems the slam-dunk logic of tying them together. Typically managers' reviews of their direct reports—and sometimes reviews of managers by their direct reports and peer reviews too—are fed into a program, and then recommended salary increases are generated according to predetermined ranges and pegged to departmental results, division results, and company results. A better performance review would seem to mean that person is worth more to the company, so why isn't that a great way to figure out what you should pay them? Apart from how ridiculously time-consuming and ineffective the annual performance review system is (about which more later), the method of calculating compensation fails to take into account some key factors that should go into salary decisions. One is how valuable the skills employees have developed while they've been working for you have become.

Account for the Value of Working for You

I didn't always think there was a way to calculate salaries other than tying pay to performance reviews. I thought the annual review and compensation-calculation process was ludicrously complex and hated doing it, but I thought it made basic sense. I was enlightened when at Netflix we started losing people recruited away with exorbitant salary offers from our competitors. One day I heard that Google had offered one of our folks almost twice his current pay, and I hit the roof.

His management panicked because he was a really important guy, and they wanted to counter. I was adamant that there was no way we were going to pay him that much. I got into a heated email exchange with his manager and a couple of VPs where I argued that "Google shouldn't decide the salaries for everybody just because they have more money than God!" We bickered about it for days, even through that whole weekend. They kept telling me, "You don't understand how good he is!" I was having none of it. But then I woke up on Sunday morning and said to myself, *Oh! Of course! No wonder Google wants him. They're right!* He had been working on some incredibly valuable personalization technology, and very few people in the world had his expertise in that area. I realized that his work with us had given him a whole new market value. I quickly fired off another email. "I was wrong, and by the way I went through the P&L and we can double the salaries of everybody in this team, and it's really fine." This experience changed our thinking about compensation. We realized that for some jobs we were creating our own expertise and scarcity, and rigidly adhering to internal salary ranges could actually be harming our best contributors financially because they could make more elsewhere. We decided that we didn't want to use a system where people had to leave to get paid what they were worth. We also encouraged our people to interview regularly. That was the most reliable and efficient way to find out how competitive our pay was.

The Value of Paying Top of Market

We also realized that setting predetermined salary ranges by marking our compensation to some percentile of the top market rate, which is a common practice, wasn't going to ensure we could hire the density of top performers we needed. We decided we would endeavor to pay top of market. Many people I consult with say they are marking their pay to market at some percentile, say the 65th. Though people sometimes think that means their company is paying 65 percent of the top market salary for a given role, what it really means is that 65 percent of people in that role industry-wide are paid less and 35 percent are paid more. That might sound good, but not only is the math questionable (because again, positions can't really be compared so strictly), but it often is not going to get you the best people you want to bring in. And it's entirely distanced from a calculation of the results you want to see. Marking to market should not mean pegging your compensation to some fixed rate vis-à-vis the overall market range; it should mean estimating the overall market value of the work a person will do for you *in the time frame that you need it done.*

People say to me all the time, "But we can't afford to pay top of market. Paying top dollar was great for Netflix; the company was booming. We're not growing that way and we don't have the margin." Fair enough. Maybe it's simply not possible, at least not in the near term, to go top of market for every position. Then I suggest identifying the positions that have the greatest potential to boost your performance and paying top of market to fill them with the very best people you can get. Think about this: what if, by paying top of market, you could bring in one supremely talented and experienced person who could do the job of two people, or even add more value than that? Consider the well-known 80/20 rule regarding sales teams, that 20 percent of your company's salespeople will generate 80 percent of your sales revenue. That rule might apply much more widely to other types of employees. I know I've seen a comparable effect in team after team.

An interesting study done by Bain and described in a *Harvard Business Review* article provides strong support for the value of this strategy. The study analyzed the distribution of talent in twenty-five global companies and found that on average, only 15 percent of employees were performance "stars." But a big difference between the most successful companies and the rest was the nature of the roles their stars were in. The authors wrote, "The best companies used intentional non-egalitarianism," meaning that "they focus their stars on areas where these individuals can have the biggest impact on company performance. As a result, the vast majority of business-critical roles—upward of 95%—are filled by A-quality talent." At the other companies, stars were distributed broadly across the departments.

Another objection I often hear to bringing in star performers at top-of-market pay is that their salaries will be so much higher than those of their new teammates. I know this type of imbalance can seem unfair. I dealt with objections to the practice at Netflix too. Say we wanted to bring in a person from another company whose salary was about twice what everybody else on the team was being paid. Department heads would sometimes ask, "Does that mean I'm paying people half of what they're worth? Are they all underpaid by 100 percent?" I'd ask back, "Well, is this new person going to be able to move us faster, maybe even twice as fast? And when we hire him, which people on your team could take his place at his former company?" The answers were usually "Well, yeah, we'll be able to move much faster" and "None of them could replace him, because they don't have his experience."

We also decided at Netflix that rather than offer new hires what would be widely deemed a reasonable increase over their pay at their former job, we would pay top of market and insist on high performance. Say a manager is interviewing two people with very similar backgrounds. The woman makes $130,000 and the man $150,000, a common discrepancy due to the long history of wage discrimination. They're comparably good. Should the manager offer them both $160,000? The answer is emphatically yes. But when I offer this advice, I often get the reaction "That's crazy! I mean, if we give her $140,000, she's going to be over the moon!" People often also respond that it would be fiscally irresponsible to spend more of the company's money than they have to. But that's if you're thinking only about keeping to a budget, rather than about the value the person will generate for you, hopefully for quite a few years beyond your current budget year. Not to mention that pegging salary offers to pay history has perpetuated the pay bias that has led to women being underpaid across so much of the workforce. That, rather than imbalances due to results contributed, is the inequity that companies should find unfair and unacceptable.

In my experience, if you focus intently on hiring the best people you can find and pay top dollar, you will almost always find that they make up *much* more in business growth than the difference in compensation.

The Magical Thinking of Signing Bonuses

Of course, one of the ways companies try to contend with market pressure to elevate compensation for key hires is bonuses, which have gotten more and more elaborate and ill-conceived.

When I was at Borland, we were hiring a guy who lived thirty miles away and the manager told me to add a relocation bonus to his offer. I said, "What?! He lives thirty miles away; he's not going to move." And the manager said, "Well, he'll like it." Sure, and people would like a new car too; does that mean you should give it to them?

Something to keep in mind: signing bonuses that you build into an offer letter, saying they are not part of the salary but a one-time signing package, thinking you've established that they won't count the next year when reviewing the person's pay, absolutely *will* count, to them. When they go from a salary of $100,000 to $120,000 and you throw in an extra $20,000, knowing full well they aren't going to use it to relocate, and then the next year you give them a 6 percent raise, so they effectively go from $140,000 to $127,200, do you think they're going to be delighted?

Transparency Helps Mark to Market

Companies tend to be adamant that salaries and other compensation should be kept confidential. One founder I consulted with told me that compensation information is like medical information. But really, it's not. One of the craziest things about companies paying so much to get salary survey data is that they usually don't share it with employees, which should be part of communicating to people why they're being compensated as they are. Companies should not be reluctant to explain their compensation rationale. They withhold the information partially because so many are following some below-top-of-market percentile rule, and they think their employees will feel they should be getting compensated at a higher overall market level. They also feel that specific individuals will react badly if they learn they're making less than colleagues they perceive to be doing work of comparable value.

No question: pay is one of people's favorite things to gripe and gossip about. But that's actually a great reason to be more transparent about it. Being open allows you to explain to people why others are being paid as they are. Having a good rationale for the discrepancy reinforces that you're a performance culture. If you don't have a rationale you can share openly with people, then you probably ought to take a hard look at why.

I've long believed that one of the best ways to ensure appropriate, well-justified compensation is to practice open dialogue about salaries and the philosophy behind them. One main reason people think that disclosing salaries would be incendiary is that compensation is so often irrational, based more on a boss liking an employee or on seniority than on contribution to results. If people are being paid based on their actual contributions, then you can say, "I know she makes $325,000 a year, and that seems disproportionate to what you make, but here are the five times that we've been in a really sticky situation where she's been crucial to getting us out. Here's the net value to the company of her good decisions." Of course, instituting such openness must be done very carefully, with good communication about why the data is being shared and about the rationale behind salaries.

So am I arguing, after all, for tying pay to performance reviews? No, I am arguing for tying pay to performance, full stop, and the way reviews are generally carried out, there is a big, big difference between those two. Perhaps the strongest testament to that is the widespread problem of women still not being paid on par with their male counterparts. Transparency would surely hasten the cure.

People love to claim that the reason Silicon Valley can't bring women's salaries over 70 percent of men's is that women don't negotiate well. I think it has more to do with both bias and the fact that women dominate HR and finance departments, roles in which people traditionally have been underpaid. The highest-paid HR person is compensated at half the typical rate of tech talent. That is partially attributable to supply and demand, given the scarcity of technical talent, but it also reflects the difficulty of attaching business results to performance in those areas. When I recommend that companies bring female salaries up to par—factoring in, of course, objective measures of results—I usually get an outcry: "We can't fix this!" I was talking to one CEO about this and he said, "My lawyers would never let me do it." I asked, "What would your lawyers be worried about?" And he said, "Well, you know that I'd get sued." I said, "You're going to give the women in your company a raise and they'll sue you? I'm thinking that probably won't happen." He responded, "No, no, no! They'd sue me because I'd be admitting I was wrong before." I said, "You are wrong!" And that is the true liability.

As for women negotiating better? Give them the information with which they can make a better case and I promise you, many, many of them will make it.

IN BRIEF

▶ The skills and talents for any given job will not match a template job description, and salaries should not be predetermined according to templates.

▶ Information from salary surveys is always behind current market conditions; do not rely on them in making salary offers.

▶ Consider not only what you can afford given your current business but also what you will be able to afford given the additional revenue a new hire might enable you to bring in.

▶ Rather than paying at some percentile of top of market, consider paying top of market, if not for all roles, then for those that are most important to your growth.

▶ Signing bonuses can lead to the impression of a salary decrease in the year after the person joins; paying the salary you need in order to bring in a top performer is the better option.

▶ Being transparent with staff about compensation encourages better judgment about salaries and undercuts biases, as well as offering the occasion for more honest dialogue about the contributions of various roles to the company's performance.

QUESTIONS TO CONSIDER

- Who on your team has grown considerably in skills and proficiency since the time they joined, and do you think you are compensating them at a level commensurate with the value they are now contributing?

- Do you know who on your team has been contacted for another job recently? Have you told all of your people that you want them to be open about discussing this?

- How much do you think being tied to predetermined salary ranges is holding you back from building the best possible team?

- What do you think your team could produce if you could hire as you'd like? Can you make that business case to management?

- If you could select certain roles for which you would make the case for hiring star performers at top-of-market compensation, which would they be and why?

- Do you regularly examine salaries for unintentional bias in pay? It doesn't have to be a big-data exercise; perhaps just a look at average pay per title for men and women.

CHAPTER EIGHT

The Art of Good Good-byes

*| Make Needed Changes Fast, and
Be a Great Place to Be From |*

We had a director of engineering at Netflix whose job was to work on improving our search capabilities, a top company priority. Streaming was taking off and we needed to be able to help people find all of our great content more easily. Facebook was also taking off at the time, and this director started making the case that we should work with Facebook and create a big presence there. He made a passionate speech about it at a company meeting. The executive team responded that Facebook wasn't one of our five priorities. Improving our search capabilities *was*, and we reiterated that it was hugely important and was what we wanted him to focus on. But he kept arguing the case about getting on Facebook, and finally I decided to talk to him about it. I told him, "Look, we all know how you feel about Facebook, but you run search. Maybe you should go work at Facebook. They'll hire you in a hot minute. We'll miss you terribly, but—call me crazy—we need the guy who's running search for us to be into search." He was brilliant, but we didn't just need someone brilliant. We needed a brilliant person in the job who really wanted to lead a team to do *that* job. Eventually he left to work at a start-up and one of his team stepped into the role and loved it.

One of the benefits of the leadership communicating clearly to everyone in the company about where you're heading and the challenges and opportunities that future will bring is that it better equips people to evaluate how well their skills fit into that future. They can also consider whether or not that future is one they want to be a part of and, if it isn't, can proactively seek out new opportunities.

Remember the engineer who kept bending my ear saying he didn't think management understood how much the nature of working at Netflix had changed from the early days? Well, the truth was that he had no interest in working for a large corporation. Meanwhile, he was located in the hotbed of bold new start-ups. Like the smart guy he was, before long he began to look around at that incredibly vibrant start-up scene and found an opportunity to work in the way that he loved so much. We should all be prepared to make moves periodically, whether within a company or to a new company, in order to work in the way we love and do things we're passionate about. We should also be told if we're not performing well enough, so that we can either make speedy corrections or move to a new firm.

Taking Performance Evaluation Ten Games at a Time

One reason the sports team analogy is so helpful in managing people is that everyone readily understands that coaches are letting the rest of the team and the fans down if they don't replace players who aren't producing top performance. Winning games is the only measure of success for sports teams, which is why it's not just players but coaches too who are replaced readily on top-performing teams.

I'm not a huge sports fan, but I can say that I've become a huge fan of good sports coaching. Since I've been out consulting, I sometimes get invited to speak with people who have coached professional sports teams. On one such occasion I found myself in Montreal getting ready to participate in a moderated discussion at the Centre Bell, which is the largest hockey arena in the world, home to the Montreal Canadiens. I was standing in a waiting area with the other person who was going to be onstage with me, Scotty Bowman, whom I'd never heard of. He's a retired National Hockey League coach who had a remarkable career, with the most wins in NHL history, coaching the Canadiens, Pittsburgh Penguins, and Detroit Red Wings, among other teams, and taking those three teams to a record nine Stanley Cup victories.

We were talking about golf and his grandkids when he pointed up at the ceiling and said, "You know, Patty, we're below the ice." I know essentially nothing about hockey, but I found it thrilling to be there with him. The moderator introduced me first, and I walked out on the stage to polite applause, a little daunted by being in this massive hockey stadium with three huge spotlights shining on me and seeing my face on a jumbotron screen the size of a billboard. Then the moderator introduced Scotty, and as he walked onstage, the crowd went absolutely wild. At that moment it sank in that he was a hockey god, and I was in this famous hockey stadium where he'd led the team to so many victories. The moderator turned to Scotty and said, "Mr. Bowman, you've coached so many famous players to such tremendous success. What's your secret? How did you give them feedback?" And Scotty said, "Well, we have an eighty-game season, and every ten games I would sit down with them individually. I'd bring all their stats and I would I ask other people—the other coaches, the other team members—for feedback also, and the player would bring a self-evaluation. Then we would have a conversation about what to do for the next ten games."

The moderator said, "Thank you, Mr. Bowman!" and then turned to me. "Patty," he said, "you're well known for not believing in the annual performance review, but I've never really heard you say what you advise instead." I pointed to Scotty and replied, "What he said!"

The problems with the annual performance review system are not just that it is rigid and has been tied too strictly to compensation decisions. It is also very time-consuming and costly. And despite the devotion of so much time and resources, it generally doesn't even do a good job of giving people the feedback and coaching they need. Too many managers rely too heavily on that once-a-year formal review to tell employees how they're performing and set goals for them. If you're a manager who has no latitude to do away with annual reviews, then fine, but go ahead and start having the kinds of frequent one-on-one meetings with your people that Scotty Bowman described. This is both much more effective and more humane. When performance issues arise, the sooner you address them with people, the better they will be able to see what they're not doing well enough and make corrections. Often, people are slammed in an annual review for some performance shortfall from many months prior. They rightfully say to themselves, *You couldn't have told me that months ago? Now you're going to give me a crappy raise, and you didn't even give me the opportunity to address this issue?*

I also believe that apprising people of how their performance is being perceived by their teammates and other colleagues is invaluable in allowing them to gain critical perspective. If negative feedback is coming from people besides the boss, it's much harder for us to fall back on the all-too-easy rationalization that the boss is just biased or has a personal problem with us.

Why Not Just Get Rid of Formal Reviews?

Consider the question I asked the chief human resources officer (CHRO) of a large corporation about its performance review process. The executive team wanted me to advise them about how to make the process more effective and efficient. I told the head of HR, who had called me, that I didn't think they would really be interested in having me work with them because I was sure they wouldn't like what I'd recommend. She pressed, and I agreed to have a one-hour call with the team. The head of IT and I were on before the others, and I asked her, "Hey, what do you think of the performance review process over there?" She said, "I hate it! I have a huge team and we're in the middle of it right now. Why do you think it took three weeks to set up this call? Nobody has time to do anything else. We've all just about stopped working on anything else but reviews. It's an insane amount of time."

When everyone was on the line, I asked my favorite question about the review process: "Do you have any proof of the value of the annual review process to your business?" As usual, they had done no analysis that could tell them the value. The bottom line for the head of HR was "Well, Patty, what we really want to know is just how to make it more efficient."

If you can't find good, solid data showing that the process is contributing to some important business metric, then I strongly advise you to lobby for doing away with it. When I advised that CHRO in our conference call to do away with the system, he responded, "Well, what else are we supposed to do?" Good question. A number of great companies, both large and small, have done away with the traditional system and instituted new approaches. Accenture, Deloitte, General Electric, and many others have concluded, just as we did at Netflix, that the review process was flawed and much too time-consuming. Many great alternatives have been developed. When I was working at Pure Software, we switched to quarterly appraisals, which were much better than annual ones. Maybe that's a good first step. One CEO I recommended this to said to me, "But I found the information from the annual review so valuable." Fine, but how much more valuable would that information be if it came more fluidly?

I understand that for many companies simply jettisoning such an elaborate process is impractical. Why not try, though, doing away with it in some tiny corner of the company and see what happens? Or you can take incremental steps. That's the way GE transitioned out of its performance review process, which it had been administering for decades. The company ran pilot programs testing changes in the system involving thirty thousand employees around the world and listening to their feedback about how to improve feedback. It then implemented a new approach with a mobile app that enables real-time feedback continuously throughout the year.

Which brings me to the other element of the prevailing

performance review process that I advise be either greatly improved or simply stopped.

RIP the PIP (or Actually Help People Improve Performance)

The conventional wisdom is that a company should put an employee it's thinking of saying good-bye to on a PIP (performance improvement plan). The way PIPs are often carried out is particularly cruel, because they're really all about proving someone is incompetent. Often the problem isn't even that a person is not a high performer or doesn't have the potential to be a high performer in another job at another company. Often there is nothing wrong with the way they work or the effort they're putting in or the way they are interacting with colleagues or their boss. They might be fabulous. They're just not right for their job as it is evolving, or they won't be high performing in the next job you need done. And there's no reason to put people who simply don't have the skills you need on a performance improvement plan.

I also came to realize that when you hire someone and it turns out that they can't do the job, the problem is with the hiring process, not the individual. You simply hired the wrong person. It's not their fault! So you shouldn't make them feel like it is.

If we think this way about who needs to move on, we can have a more honest conversation with people that's not about casting aspersions on them. There is no need to essentialize them as a failure. We should simply be pointing out that they're not a good match for what we need. It's not personal and it's not about failure. It's about aligning skills and know-how with the team objectives. That doesn't mean that people won't be disappointed or sad or unhappy or upset. I've wept through as many good-byes as anybody else. But ultimately people understand, and they appreciate that you're not lying to them.

For much of my career in HR, I spent lots of time on PIPs. I do think that they have the potential to work well, about which more in a bit. But when I started working closely with programming teams at Netflix, I came to understand that sometimes it's in everyone's interest for people to move on to a new job quickly rather than keep trying to improve their performance. I saw a few teams late to deliver again and again, and I realized that it wasn't because people weren't working hard; they were working their asses off. They just didn't know what they were doing! Yes, sometimes managers and colleagues can teach people, but often it's vital to efficiently find people who can do the work *now*. And prolonging efforts to help people improve often simply impedes them from making true progress—at another firm.

One of the teams at Netflix hired a guy that everyone loved. I was pretty sure after interviewing him that we should keep looking for a more qualified person. But the team said, "No! We'll teach him; we'll get him up to speed." I said, "Maybe, but you'll get him up to speed for what we need now, not six months from now." They insisted. Six months later the poor guy was even further behind the curve and his team was totally frustrated and also crazy busy making up for his shortfall. Meanwhile, I was able to call the HR person at Apple, whom I knew pretty well, and recommend him, and he had a great new job there even before he left. He came into my cubicle on his last day and gave me a big flowering bush, God love him.

There are certainly many cases in which the PIP process

could be used to help someone make vital improvements in performance. That should absolutely be the only goal of the process. If there is a clear way to assist a person in getting up to speed with a skill or set of skills in a reasonable period of time, I say, wonderful, do that. Those skills might not be nuts-and-bolts job requirements like learning a new program or becoming proficient in giving presentations. They might be more qualitative, "soft" skills like becoming a better team player or learning how to manage people better. I saw many employees considerably improve their people skills. The key is to be realistic about how likely it is that significant improvement can be made. And be sure that improvement is the true goal, rather than making a case to let someone go. If it's not, then the responsible thing to do is to forgo the process.

People Very Rarely Sue

Many people push back with me about getting rid of the PIP process because they think it's a requirement to avoid being sued. I don't think people realize how hard it is to actually sue a company and how much time it takes—in many cases years. In my experience, people sue their former employers because they think they've been treated unfairly. But that's not because they weren't put on an improvement plan. It's generally because they weren't told the truth when they should have been about their performance or their fit. I've found that generally if people are mad enough to sue, there was a point when somebody should have told them, "You know, you're being a jerk! You're making us crazy! We're not going to want you around anymore if you keep treating people like that." Or if the situation was that the future looked significantly different from the present, no one said, "I want you to know that in six months this is what success is going to look like. It's very different from what we're doing now. It's going to require significantly different sets of experiences and really different ways of doing things. And if I were recruiting for this team from scratch, I'm not sure I'd hire you." That conversation might be painful, but it's truthful, and it allows you both to do a better job of assessing whether or not a person will be able to adapt, or even wants to adapt. Often people are well aware that they're not getting the job done right, and that's no fun for them at all. Talking openly about the problem is a relief. One person said to me after his manager had told him we had to let him go, "Well, he gave me enough rope to hang myself and I did it twice; tell him that he could have actually shortened the rope by half, because I knew fifty feet ago."

The irony of the PIP being used as a means to avoid being sued is that it actually fans the flames of resentment, all because of the fear of being honest.

About "Engagement"

"Engagement" is a term that, when used in business, I dislike about as just about as much as "empowerment." In a talk I gave at a conference to a room full of just HR people, I asked them, "How many of you have laid anybody off?" Everybody's hand went up. Then I asked, "Okay, how many of you have laid off a family member?" Zero hands. "And yet," I said, "how many of you use the word 'family' at work every day?"

For so much of my traditional HR life, a huge part of my work was relationship therapy. People constantly wanted me to facilitate counseling sessions with bosses and employees. Eventually I stopped agreeing to do them because every time I tried to intervene, it backfired. What is essential, instead, is to coach not only managers but all employees that they are expected to communicate openly about issues they are having with one another.

Another reason I hate the word "engagement" as we use it about work life is that it implies that the problem in performance is generally that people aren't committed to their jobs. Let's face it: such people are low-hanging fruit. If all high performance required was letting go of people who aren't engaged, every company would be thriving.

I recently had a conversation with a brilliant new head of HR that's a cautionary tale about focusing so much on engagement. She'd been at her new company for eight weeks, and she had already conducted a seriously eye-opening analysis of how employee engagement tracked with performance. She had taken a close look at the company's heat-mapping survey, which measured how happy and engaged employees were, and compared those results with the performance of teams. The good news, she told me, was that most of the company was green, meaning highly engaged and happy. But the bad news was that the teams with subpar performance were just as green as those that were performing really well. That's a striking demonstration that there is not such a simple link between engagement and performance. By superimposing business metrics over happiness metrics, she enabled the company to begin to differentiate much more effectively what was going on in the teams that were performing so well versus those that weren't.

In my experience, high performers are, in fact, often somewhat frustrated with how their teams are performing rather than satisfied that everything is going swimmingly and life is all good. They are pushing for great results, and achieving those often requires some pain and a degree of discontent. That commitment to achievement is what we want to foster, not the expectation that as long as you're working hard, the company will have your back.

We should not make false promises of job security. I was consulting to a CEO and he asked me, "What should I do about our call center people? We've moved the rest of the company into a new building, and I don't think we want to bring our call center people into the space. I think it might be best to outsource that work now." I asked him, "Why have you been lying to them?" He said, "What are you talking about? I would never do that! Never in a million years!" So I asked him, "Is it true that you said that everybody who comes to work for you will have a future in the company, that their career with the company will continue as long as they're willing to contribute?" He said, "Yeah, I said that, but that was a few years ago!" And I said, "Well, your recruiters are quoting you and still saying it every day." False promises will only lead to people feeling betrayed.

People often come up to me after a talk to ask for career guidance. I tell them, "You want to be a lifelong learner; you want to always be acquiring new skills and having new experiences, and that doesn't have to be at the same company. The fact is that sometimes you're hired by a company to do something, and then you do it and it's done. If I hire people to rebuild my garage, when they're done I don't need them to rebuild the back of my house."

My Algorithm

I tell managers to use a simple rule when evaluating their teams, which I call an algorithm because engineers love the word, and I love engineers: is what this person loves to do, that they're extraordinarily good at doing, something we need someone to be great at?

This way of thinking is just like reasoning about any other business activity. It's based on critical thinking and it takes the emotion out of the decision. Employees can also use the algorithm to assess whether they should stay at a company or start looking for a new job that will be a better fit.

Another good thing about it is that it helps hiring managers to appreciate what a person's talents and passions are, rather than fixating on what they can't do, and to assist them in finding a better fit in a next job. Another crazy traditional HR rule is that managers should not give references to people who are fired. This too is out of fear of being sued. But you can be open with people about what sort of reference you'll be able to give and let them decide.

I used to sit down with my soon-to-be-ex-employees and say, "Okay, we've established the fact that you're not a team leader"— for example—"but that's okay, you're a really talented engineer. I'll be happy to be a reference for your technical acumen, but I'm not a good choice if you need praise about your management skills."

As with the programmer I helped get a job at Apple, I actively recommended people who were leaving us to other companies. Many have gone on to have flourishing careers elsewhere. They shouldn't have to carry with them the stigma of being "fired." When someone is "fired," no weapons are involved; they're not being killed. And who first decided to say that people were being "terminated"? One company's failure might be another company's treasure. Many times I found that even people I thought were not very good went on to be really successful because they found the right fit.

One of my favorite cases of someone finding a really great new fit is a designer whom I just loved. She'd been with Netflix since the very early days and had weathered so many changes.

She worked like a demon, and she was very talented, but as the product became more and more about a different kind of design, her skills were no longer a good match. It was so hard to let her go, and I told her, "Don't lose me, okay? I'm there if you ever need me." Well, she moved right on to a great new job at one of the best companies in Silicon Valley. Then one day I was meeting with the head of HR at Microsoft, and while I was sitting in the lobby, this designer walked by. I called out, "Girl, what are you doing here?" And she told me she was interviewing for another job. We had a great catch-up, and when the HR head showed up, the designer and I gave each other a big hug. As I was walking away with the HR head, she said to me, "Hey, I understand that you have a practice of proactively letting people go and that you often stay close with them. How do you do that? Tell me about somebody you fired who you're still on good terms with." I said, "Well, the woman you just saw me with is somebody I had to let go." She said, "She hugged you!" And I told her, "Yeah, I loved her then and I still do!

Owning and Living the Culture

There is no question that the discipline of proactively letting people go was one of the hardest, probably the single hardest, component of the Netflix culture for managers to become comfortable with. But most of them did.

John Ciancutti, one of my favorite Netflix alumni, was beautifully clear about how he experienced this transformation. He told me, "The way that we're socialized to work with people, to not tell them hard truths, is completely different from how Netflix was trying to get us to operate, and so you're fighting your own instincts. And for me I really learned to embrace the model at Netflix after I hired a guy who was super strong on paper and knocked it out of the park in the interview, but he could just not execute in the Netflix environment at all well. He wasn't a strong doer, and at Netflix it wasn't enough to be smart; you had to get a lot done. Learning to come to grips with that and say good-bye to him, even though he was very popular, was owning the culture, and having that confidence from letting him go was the point for me when I never looked back."

Jessica Neal, who was our VP of staffing, moved on from Netflix and is working with a great start-up, Scopely, where the CEO is really innovative and wants to build a freedom-and-responsibility culture, and she's helping managers learn the beauty of proactively strengthening their teams. She told me that some of their teams were doing good but not great work, and she helped the team leaders see that they had to make changes. She said, "They come to me and say, 'Oh my God, my team meetings are better. We move faster. I didn't realize how much weight it was.'"

One of my fondest moments at Netflix was right before I left, when a VP, Kevin McEntee, whom I hadn't seen in quite a while, scheduled a meeting with me. When I asked him what was up, he said he was going to let go one of his team leaders who'd been with the company for a long time but was doing work we had been phasing out. Then he told me, "I've talked to her, we've been discussing it for the last couple of months, so she knows it's coming. We're going to make her last day Friday, and I'm going to talk to her about ten o'clock in the morning. Then I'll have her come see you because I know she's going to want to say good-bye. Then I'm going to gather the rest of her team in person and talk to them about it. I'll send an email to all the other teams after that, and tonight I'll tell the rest of management teams so they won't be surprised. I know what we're going to tell people: how great she was and that she's done and she's moving on." When he finished, I just said, "Glad I could help!" He laughed and said, "Yeah, I don't know why I came in here." And I said, "No, it's great. It makes me really proud that you've done this all on your own."

The next week another manager came to me and said, "I have this problem person on my team," and I told him he should go and talk to Kevin. He pushed back and said, "But I came to you." I told him, "You know, you'll learn more about how it really works in our culture by talking to another leader."

Instilling belief in the practice gets easier as managers come on board. The greater the density of great team builders you achieve, the more you can spread the practice organically.

Living It Myself

I'm not advocating this only as one who has seen the positive results for others; I've also gone through the process of recognizing that it was time to proactively move on, as I did when I jumped over to Pure to work with Reed. I've also had to move on when doing so was very difficult for me. Eventually, when we worked together at Netflix, Reed and I both had to come to terms with the fact that it was time for me to go. Like anyone who has worked hard and helped to build something they are proud of, I found the thought of leaving painful. Walking away from an exciting future that I wouldn't be part of was perhaps the most difficult part. I had experienced this many, many times from the other side of the table. I was not immune to the emotion of the situation. But I had tremendous respect for Reed's discipline to choose his team for the future.

I absolutely loved my fourteen years at Netflix, and I am proud of, and gratified by, all that we accomplished—especially how we built the culture. But I am also now loving the opportunity to share the insights I learned with other companies, particularly with so many creative and brilliant start-up founders. Just as I have seen with so many of the Netflixers who have moved on to new challenges, I am thrilled to be applying the lessons I learned to help other dynamic organizations figure out the way forward.

And Reed and I have had a very good good-bye. We had a wild and exhilarating ride, and we are forever friends. I still say "we" when I refer to Netflix and probably always will. This book of advice is a direct result of my experience and experiments there. I will always follow the success of the company and the people in it. As I see Netflix win so many awards and become part of the entertainment landscape, I could not be more delighted. Netflix is not about to stop moving on with moving on, and neither am I.

Much media coverage of the labor market in recent years has mourned the passing of lifetime employment. There is no question that the dislocations of the contemporary work world can be horribly stressful and inflict terrible costs on employees and their families, or that they have left far too many people behind. The loss of purposeful and rewarding employment by so many skilled and hardworking individuals is a tragedy that the business community and our politicians must find much more effective ways of redressing. The best way for both companies and individuals to contend with the fierce competitive dynamism of business today is to stay limber, to make sure they are developing the skills and gaining the experience required for future success. We should all be proactively preparing for the road ahead.

Managers don't do best by their people by sugarcoating difficult truths, waiting until the last moment to let them go, or shunting them into roles they don't truly want or the company doesn't really need. The effects of all of these are disempowering, dispiriting, and corrosive, both for the individuals in question and for entire teams. People deserve to know the truth of their prospects, in real time. Being totally honest with them and supporting them in finding new opportunities is the best way to ensure that both they and your team can flourish.

• • •

It takes practice and courage to get better at truth. It takes finding your personal power. You never really finish this task, so it's time to get started!

IN BRIEF

► Employees need to be able to see whether their talents and passions are a good match for the future you are heading to, in order to determine whether they may be a better fit at another firm.

► People should hear frequently about how well they're performing. Even if doing away with the annual performance process is not feasible for you, institute much more frequent meetings to discuss performance.

► If doing away with the annual review process is an option for you, try it! The process is a big waste of time and can become a stand-in for real-time information about performance.

► Either make performance improvement plans genuine efforts to help people improve performance or get rid of them.

► The chances you'll get sued by an employee who is let go are vanishingly slim, especially if you have been responsibly and regularly sharing with that person the problems you perceive with their performance.

▶ The focus on employee engagement is misplaced; there is not necessarily a correlation between high engagement and high performance. There is also not necessarily a correlation between high performance in a current job and high performance in the job of the future.

▶ Use my algorithm in making personnel decisions: Is what this person loves to do, that they're extraordinarily good at doing, something we need someone to be great at?

▶ All managers can actively help their exiting team members find great new opportunities; good-byes can be very good.

▶ Managers who adopt this more fluid approach to performance review and team building come to clearly see that it is better for all concerned and better for overall team performance.

QUESTIONS TO CONSIDER

- What would be the equivalent for you of offering your team members individual general feedback on their performance ten games at a time?

- Might it make sense to determine feedback frequency based on benchmark deadlines for achieving team goals, rather than according to a set time period? That might, for example, mean timing discussions according to the stages of completion for a project.

- Whom on other teams could you ask to provide feedback about your team members' performance?

- Can you say that every person on your team is doing a job they're passionate about and great at and that you need them to be doing? If not, can you have a conversation with those who aren't about other opportunities in the company they could consider or about the landscape of opportunity they can consider outside?

- Are you building a network of managers at other firms to whom you can recommend your exiting team members?

- How well are you keeping up on changes in business operations and personnel at firms that might offer good opportunities for them?

Conclusion

The distinctive, explicitly articulated, and appealing culture at Netflix helped our hiring managers and my team consistently recruit great people, even in the face of extremely fierce competition. When I talked with my former VP of HR Jessica Neal about this, she said a great thing about what a company's culture should be: "Culture is the strategy of how you work. And if people believe it is a strategy and that it is important, they will help you think about it deeply and try things."

She has been in the process of adapting the Netflix culture to the start-up she joined, and she shared a wonderful insight about the process: "You can't do it all at once; you have to pick where you want to start, prioritizing just as you do with the rest of the business." That takes me back to my point about approaching people management the way we approach product management. We took things a step at a time at Netflix. We tested. We made some mistakes. We rethought and tried again. We were working actively on developing the culture throughout the fourteen years I was there, and I'm sure Reed and his team are not about to stop.

The most gratifying thing about consulting has been learning how hungry so many organizational leaders are for a new way to work, from twenty-person start-ups to a nonprofit foundation to one the oldest and most august public relations firms. I recently gave a talk to a group of executives at J. Walter Thompson. The 152-year-old company had just won an award for an edgy television ad for Coca-Cola. In it, a teenage girl looks out her kitchen window, mooning over the hunky young pool guy, while her gay brother does the same from his bedroom window upstairs. They both rush to bring the pool guy a can of Coke, only to discover that their cougar mother has beat them to it. That ad, I discovered, was made by the company's Argentina group, a scrappy, relatively small unit that was hungry and lean and felt free to push the envelope. The CEO, Tamara Ingram, who invited me to come, wants to be sure the company keeps fostering that kind of creative risk taking. A comment she made to me after the talk speaks to my hopes for sharing my experiences in culture building: "The telling of what you've accomplished has really helped us see how we could do things differently."

The process is evolutionary, and as with evolution in nature, some changes won't be adaptive and you'll have to try again. Some people will find the changes uncomfortable. People will push back, and some may decide to leave. Some of the practices that worked so well at Netflix might not work for you, or at least not right away. I'm constantly helping founders and CEOs plan how they can begin implementing change in the ways that will work best for them, so they can create their own version of a freedom and responsibility culture.

Experimenting incrementally and allowing for variations on the themes is vital. Different team leaders may adapt the practices in different ways. Teams—and whole departments—

can have their own cultures as well as incorporating common fundamental precepts. Another thing I loved that Jessica said was that the Netflix culture "lived across the company." As different as the engineering culture was from the marketing culture and the culture of the content creators in LA, we were all ultimately unified around our fundamentals.

One thing I absolutely advise is making sure your HR people are your partners; you must stress to them that you want them to be true business-building partners. When your HR people are businesspeople first, it doesn't seem odd to the rest of your management team to have them in the room for a staff meeting or to coach hiring managers about how to interview and give people feedback. Instead of thinking HR is there to catch them misbehaving, team leaders will open up to input. Make sure they really know how your business operates. Do they know your three key drivers of revenue? Do they know who your top four competitors are? Do they know about the technology that's about to disrupt your market? Tell them. If they don't want to know, replace them.

Another foundation of successful culture change is honesty about the challenges and the nature of progress along the way. In one of our company meetings, when Reed was taking questions, someone stood up and said, "I think it's time to address the culture of fear." This was when we were facing the huge downturn in the economy following the dot-com boom. People expected layoffs and we had been totally clear that they could happen. The guy standing up had given a presentation earlier that day about how we were not going to make tiny changes in the Netflix product; we were going mountain climbing, up big mountains. Reed picked up the metaphor. He said maybe some fear isn't so bad. When you're taking on a mountain the magnitude of Mt. Fuji or K2, you have to bring oxygen. It's scary. But if you go up and a storm comes, you can go back to base camp, and nobody's going to tell you that you're a failure. I loved that because it expressed so well that not only were we engaged in a great challenge, which would involve setbacks, but we were also on a great adventure.

One thing I can promise you about the process of building your own culture of freedom and responsibility is that you will be heartened by how people step up. When people feel that they have more power, more control over their careers, they feel more confidence—confidence to speak up more, to take more risks, to pick themselves up again when they make mistakes, and to take on more and more responsibility. They will amaze you. Just imagine if you had an organization full of people who know they have power. Think of the better judgments they'll make and how much faster they will make them. Think of how they'll surprise you with ideas you could never have asked them for. Imagine what it will be like to be so much more honest and open—you with them and them with you.

Keep reminding yourself that people *have* power. It's not your job to give it to them. Appreciate their power, unleash it from hidebound policies, approvals, and procedures, and trust me, they will be powerful.

Notes

Page 22, Reportedly 78 percent: American Express, "Good Service Is Good Business: American Consumers Willing to Spend More with Companies That Get Service Right, According to American Express Survey," news release, May 3, 2011, http://about.americanexpress.com/news/pr/2011/csbar.aspx.

Page 22, estimated at $62 billion annually: NewVoiceMedia, "The $62 Billion Customer Service Scared Away," NewVoice Media.com, May 24, 2016, www.newvoicemedia.com/en-us/news/the-62-billion-customer-service-scared-away.

Page 22, Research also shows: Better Business Bureau, "Negative Reviews: A Golden Opportunity for Business," September 14, 2014, www.bbb.org/phoenix/news-events/business-tips/2014/09/negative-reviews-a-golden-opportunity-for-business/.

Page 43, A study by Deloitte: Mark J. Cotteleer and Timothy Murphy, "Ignoring Bad News: How Behavioral Factors Influence Us to Sugarcoat or Avoid Negative Messages" (white paper,

Deloitte University Press, 2015), https://dupress.deloitte.com/content/dam/dup-us-en/articles/business-communications-strategies/DUP_1214_IgnoringBadNews.pdf, page 10.

Page 45, This may be why: Halley Bock, "Why Honesty Is the Secret Ingredient of Successful Organizations," Conference-Board.org, June 14, 2013, www.conference-board.org/blog/post.cfm?post=1897.

Page 117, An interesting study: Michael Mankins, "The Best Companies Don't Have More Stars—They Cluster Them Together," *Harvard Business Review*, Febuary 3, 2017, https://hbr.org/2017/02/the-best-companies-dont-have-more-stars-they-cluster-them-together.

In Gratitude

Without the Silicon Guild coming up with an innovative alternative to traditional book publishing, this never would have happened. Peter Sims not only convinced me that I had a message but was instrumental in talking me through the first chapters, encouraging me along the way, and introducing me to Emily Loose.

Emily, my editor and so much more: together we turned my words and stories into the message I needed to say. Literally, I wouldn't have a book without you.

Piotr Juszkiewicz, my publisher: your steady, constant encouragement, nagging, honesty, and friendship made this book come to be.

Thanks also to Hilary Roberts for the fabulous copyediting and to Loraine Perez for helping my life stay organized.

A number of people took the time to review early drafts of the book. An especially big thank you to Tom Rath for his valuable insights and ideas, and to David Martin, Ted Swann, Larry Dlugosh, Ori Brafman, Laura Mion, LeeAnn Mallorie, Maria De Guzman, Charles Dimmler, Gabrielle Toledano,

Nathan Vogt, Eric Kettunen, Keith Arsenault, Frank Fritsch, Aileen Garcia, Jessica Krakoski, Matthew Rosebaugh, Barbara Henricks, Yongwei Yang, and Dennis Doerfl.

Through my decades-long working relationship with Reed Hastings, I learned to question everything and to think like an innovator. Netflix was the best laboratory ever. Special thanks to all the Netflix employees past and present for their constant focus on company culture and collaboration and for letting me share some of their stories.

My mom and my sister are constant models of powerful women. My kids, Tristan, Franny, and Rose, have inspired me to influence the future of work for them.

Lastly, Michael Chamberlain, thanks for believing in me.